College Transfer Success

2nd edition, 2014

Published by CPCC Press
PO Box 35009
Charlotte, NC 28235
cpccpress@cpcc.edu

ISBN: 978-1-59494-064-4

Published and Printed in the United States of America

For additional information, you are invited to contact:

Alyssa Williams & Donna Housman
Central Piedmont Community College
P.O. Box 35009
Charlotte, N.C. 28235-5009

Tel: 704.330.6357 or 704.330.4854
E-mail: alyssa.williams@cpcc.edu or donna.housman@cpcc.edu
Website: www.cpcc.edu
            www.cpccpress.com

CPCC Press is a division of Central Piedmont Community College Services Corporation.

Copyright © 2014 by CPCC Press, PO Box 35009, Charlotte, NC 28235; 704.330.6731; www.cpccservicescorporation.com.

Table of Contents

AUTHORS

Alyssa Bethel Williams, MA is a faculty member at Central Piedmont Community College in Charlotte, N.C. She has more than 17 years of experience as an instructor, advisor and trainer of adults in the public, private and community college sectors of higher education.

Her areas of collegiate experience include leadership development, career counseling, new student orientation, academic advising, residence life, Greek affairs, judicial affairs, services for students with disabilities and programming.

She is a graduate of Tusculum College and received a master's degree in Student Development for Higher Education from Trinity University. In her current role, she is an instructor and discipline chair for Career Assessment and Transfer Student Success courses, and teaches College Student Success and College Study Skills courses. Alyssa has also trained adults in the corporate arena on effective leadership, team building, group facilitation, diversity and conflict mediation and resolution.

Donna Housman, MS is a faculty member at Central Piedmont Community College. She has more than 20 years of experience in teaching and training adults in corporate, academic and public settings, focusing on leadership and management development, facilitation skills, self-awareness and team building.

She is a graduate of Wake Forest University and has a master's degree in Adult Education from Virginia Polytechnic Institute and State University. In her current role, she teaches College Study Skills, Career Assessment, College Transfer Success and College Student Success.

She also previously taught English as a Second Language (ESL) classes, providing civics-based ESL instruction for intermediate and advanced ESL students, and she has served as an instructor for ESL Fast Track Teacher Training.

Acknowledgments

This textbook is a project that would not have been possible without the guidance, support, encouragement, feedback and contributions of many individuals. These individuals selflessly extended their valuable **assistance** in the preparation and completion of this **project**.

First, we are grateful to our students. Your commitment to your academic and career pursuits inspired us to pursue this project in a way that would have a significant impact on your matriculation. We endeavor to provide you with information and skills that will create an impetus for your successful transfer to a four-year college/university.

We would like to thank our proof readers, Owen Sutkowski, Adam Hypes, Kelly DeMarte and Maria Williams from the Central Piedmont Community College Transfer Resource Center. We sincerely appreciate your willingness to share your experience, insight and feedback. Your contributions were invaluable to this effort.

Also, we would like to acknowledge, with appreciation, Erin Phillips and Stephen Lancaster from the Financial Aid/Veterans Affairs department for their assistance.

Finally, we would like to express our gratitude to the CPCC ACA Division. Your support and encouragement was essential to the development of this textbook. Thank you for being the catalyst through which we could express our vision. We are grateful to be a part of such a wonderful team.

We hope this textbook will serve as an intrinsic framework that will enable students to address and take onus of both the conceptual and process elements of transfer admission and degree completion at a four-year college/university. Our goal is to promote the student's ability to embrace the integration of the academic and student support environments of a college to bring about successful degree completion and readiness for the professional arena.

Thanks to each of you for your contributions that have helped shape this textbook.

Alyssa Bethel Williams
Donna Dimsdale Housman

Introduction

Congratulations on making the decision to continue your education after your community college experience is complete. You have made a wise decision! Research shows the higher your level of education, the lower your unemployment and the higher your earnings will be.

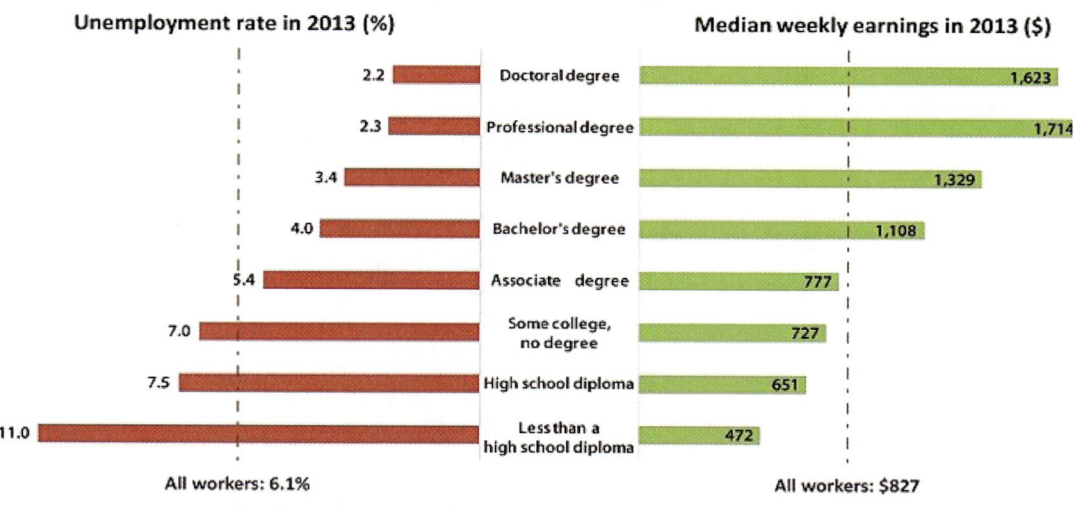

Earnings and unemployment rates by educational attainment

Unemployment rate in 2013 (%)	Educational attainment	Median weekly earnings in 2013 ($)
2.2	Doctoral degree	1,623
2.3	Professional degree	1,714
3.4	Master's degree	1,329
4.0	Bachelor's degree	1,108
5.4	Associate degree	777
7.0	Some college, no degree	727
7.5	High school diploma	651
11.0	Less than a high school diploma	472

All workers: 6.1%   All workers: $827

Note: Data are for persons age 25 and over. Earnings are for full-time wage and salary workers.
Source: Current Population Survey, U.S. Bureau of Labor Statistics, U.S. Department of Labor

Today in the United States more than 45 percent of college students start in a community college (O'Shaughnessy, 2008). Here are some of the benefits of starting at a community college:

- The cost of attending a community college is less expensive than attending a college or university.
- The community college provides great experiential training before going to a four-year university.
- Community college classes are smaller and students can receive more individual attention.
- Students at a community college may be offered priority admissions to four-year colleges/universities.
- Community colleges boast great accessibility and flexibility that allow students to live at home, work and save money.
- If necessary, students can overcome academic deficiencies and become better prepared for college-level work at a community college.

Many community college students are better prepared to transfer to a four-year college or university after earning a two-year degree or satisfying their general education requirements.

When a high school student decides to attend college, there is a defined process and plan in terms of college preparation and selection. But as a transfer student, there is not a "one size fits all" approach. Don't worry! In this course we will answer many of your questions and go through a systematic process to help you with the successful transition to a four-year college or university.

The "ACA College Transfer Success" was created to assist students in their successful transfer from a community college to a senior institution. It will provide information and strategies necessary to develop clear academic and professional goals beyond the community college experience. Topics include the Comprehensive Articulation Agreement (CAA), college culture, paying for college, course planning, student affairs, career exploration, researching information on senior institutions, strategic planning, critical thinking and communication skills for a successful academic transition.

Whatever your situation, this textbook will help you answer questions such as:

- When and how do I start planning for transfer?
- How do I know the best college to choose for my major?
- What things do I need to consider to ensure a proper fit for me culturally, socially and academically?
- What are the admission requirements to the school?
- Will they accept the courses I have already taken for credit toward an advanced degree?
- What financial aid or scholarships might be available to me?

Transferring successfully from your community college will require you to answer these questions and many others. You will have the opportunity to consider what college will meet your personal, social, academic, financial and cultural needs, which brings us to the learning outcomes for this course.

The Student Learning Outcomes for the course are:

1. Demonstrate the basic skills necessary to research senior institutions and develop a strategic plan for completing community college academic goals, including certificates, diplomas, and/or associate degrees.

2. Demonstrate an ability to identify the rights and responsibilities of transfer students under the Comprehensive Articulation Agreement (CAA), including Universal General Education Transfer Component (UGETC) designated courses, the Transfer Assured Admissions Policy (TAAP), the CAA appeals process and university tuition surcharge.

3. Develop a strategic plan for successfully transferring to a university and preparing for a new career.

4. Evaluate learning strategies, including note-taking, test-taking, information processing, time management, and memorization techniques, and identify strategies for improvement.

5. Identify essential college resources, including financial aid, advising, registration, tutoring, library services, computer labs, and counseling services and recognize the importance of these resources to student success.

6. Identify essential college policies and procedures, including academic integrity such as avoiding plagiarism, calculating a GPA, and maintaining satisfactory academic progress for financial aid eligibility and/or good academic standing.

Throughout the course we will refer to the *5 Steps for Transfer Success*. They are listed on the next page and will be a road map to guide us as we move through the course.

The 5 Steps to Transfer Success

Step 1: Choosing the Right Major for Your Career
- Self-Assessment
- Choosing Your Major

Step 2: Understanding College Culture and Your Personal Needs
- Researching Different Types of Colleges/Universities in the U.S.
- Exploring Your Individual College Needs
- Investigating the Best Colleges for Your Career Choice and Major
- Investigating Degree Requirements
- Understanding Course Planning and the CAA

Step 3: Researching Finance Options to Pay for Your Four-Year College
- Exploring the Cost of College
- Investigating Different Sources Available to Pay for College
- Researching Ways to Save on College Cost
- Creating a Plan for Paying for College

Step 4: Creating a Personal Admissions Campaign
- Researching Admission Requirements
- Conducting Information Interviews
- Understanding Admission Requirements
- Conducting College Interviews/Campus Visits
- Creating an Admissions Tracking System and Timeline
- Completing Your Transfer and Financial Aid Applications

Step 5: Making Your Choice and Making the Transition
- Evaluating Your Choices
- Identifying a Plan B
- Accepting Your Final Offer
- Making the Transition Successfully

How to Use this Textbook

"The information contained in this workbook is essential to navigating the transfer process. No matter where a student is on their path to a four-year degree, there are resources within this guide to assist and support their transition." – Owen Sutkowski, MS, Director of Transfer and Career Services at Central Piedmont Community College

This textbook was developed to help guide you through your journey as you transfer from a community college to a senior institution. It will provide information and strategies necessary to develop clear academic and professional goals beyond the community college experience.

In this guide you will find narratives and exercises to walk you through the specific steps of choosing your major, understanding college culture, researching prospective colleges and then making your choices. There are also references to online resources and books that will be useful in your process.

We hope this textbook will be a close companion as you work your way through this course and this life decision.

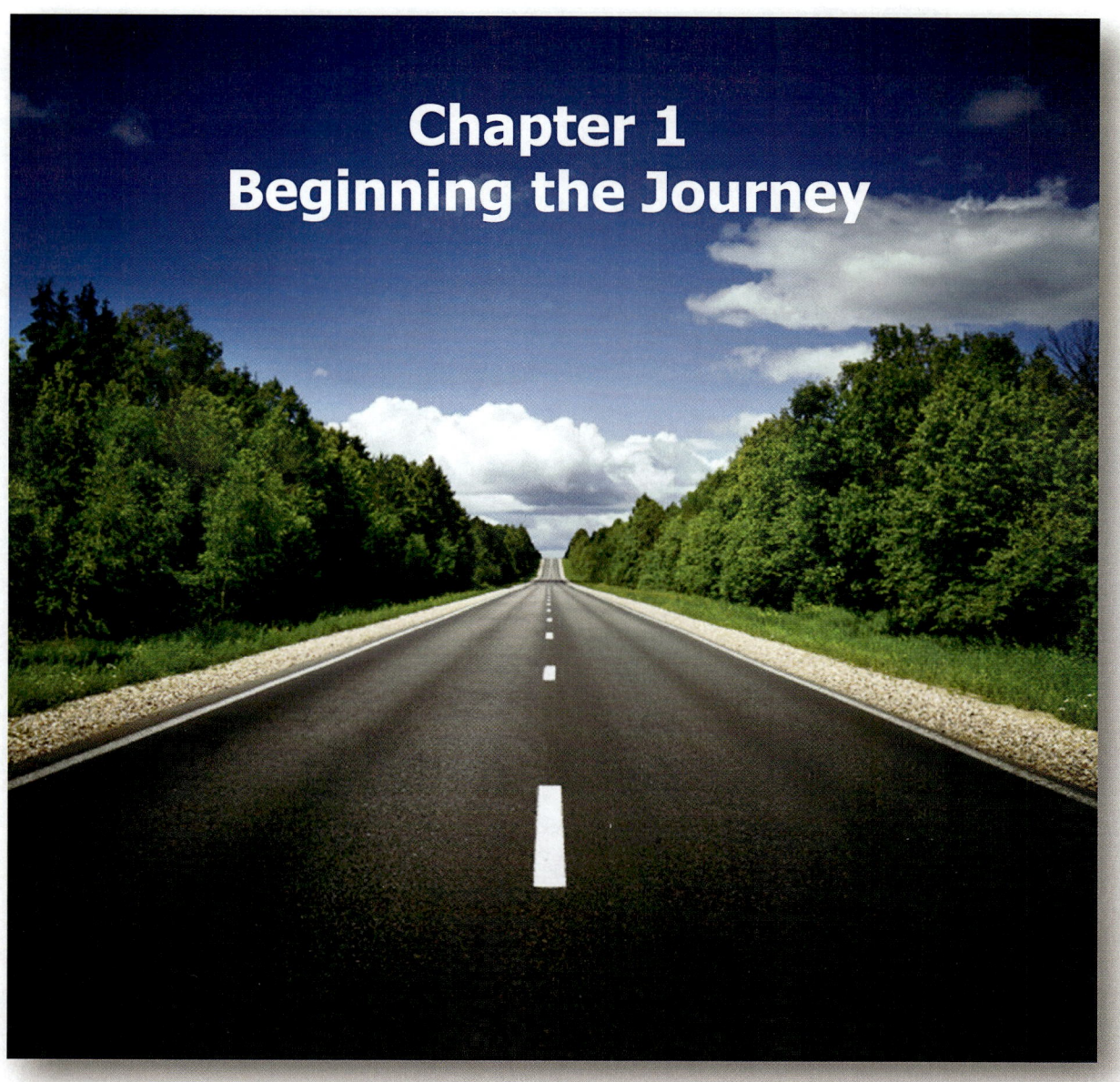

Chapter 1
Beginning the Journey

"A happy life is one which is in accord with its own nature." — Seneca

In this chapter you will:
✔ Assess Yourself
✔ Choose Your Major

Self Assessment

College is a place where you will discover who you are, what you value, what you want out of life and ultimately who you want to be when you "grow up." This can only be described as a journey of self-discovery and exploration. One of the things you need to do before you transfer to a four-year college or university is choose a major, and the first step in choosing your major is knowing yourself.

This chapter is designed to assist you in the process of choosing the right major for you. To do this, you will start by assessing yourself, evaluating options and selecting your major. This does not have to be an overwhelming experience. The activities in this chapter will help you explore what options exist.

Why It's Important

You are getting ready to make one of the most important decisions of your life: What you will choose for a career and where you will transfer to complete your education so you are ready to start this new chapter of your life.

There are undoubtedly many people who have given you advice or expressed their expectations of you up to this point in your life. This advice was probably beneficial in getting you to where you are today; but now, it is up to you.

- What do you want?
- What will help you achieve your goals?
- What will give you personal and professional satisfaction?

The first step is to know yourself. A clear, true assessment of who you are will help guide you in choosing the right major for your career and point you toward prospective colleges that can help you reach your goals.

Making sure there is congruency between your personality and career choice is one of the most important things you can do to ensure career happiness and success. If you like to be around people and you are sitting at your computer all day alone, this is not a good match! There are many facets to knowing yourself. These include looking at your skills, interests, personality and values.

In his text "The Pathfinder," Nicholas Lore expresses a concept called the "Right Livelihood." This is an ancient Asian philosophical concept that proposes a perfect working relationship and flow between you and the world around you. "Your work fully expresses all aspects of your nature. It fits your innate talents perfectly. It expresses your temperament and personality. It provides the rewards that matter to you. It fulfills your goals. It occurs in an environment that is suitable and appropriate to who you are." (Lore, 1998) It is when you are being you.

Ways to Assess Yourself

There are many ways to assess yourself and learn more about your skills, talents and personality. These may vary depending on what decisions you have already made, how sure you are about these decisions and what issues you still need assistance with.

Check with your community college to see if they offer a career development program for students that can help you make a career decision with the assistance of a trained career counselor. These programs will help you explore and gather information about yourself and future careers, so you may make an informed choice about your best career match. You will discuss your goals and expectations; use assessments to generate lists of careers; define your skills; interests and personality; and discover what you are passionate about.

Many career development programs offer career assessments such as the Myers-Briggs Type Indicator® or The Strong Interest Inventory®. Each assessment has its own advantages. The Myers-Briggs Type Indicator® will identify your personality type and provide a list of career fields that people with your personality type often pursue. The Strong Interest Inventory® asks questions about academic subjects and activities you enjoy and then compares your responses to people in various career fields to look for similarities. You can also access interactive free assessments through CFNC (College Foundation of North Carolina) that incorporate career information with career assessment.

Learning about yourself and your style is important not only in your college and career decisions, but also in your relationships with family, friends, instructors and work colleagues. Being self-aware takes courage and the ability to see things about yourself that you may not like. It also gives you so many opportunities to live a life that is deeper, richer and more authentic. It can bring you contentment and purpose. Let's get started!

Choosing Your Major

Separating Myth From Reality

The "Major" Myth: Most college students think there is a corresponding academic major for each specific career field, and that it's impossible to enter most career fields unless they choose that matching major as a student. This is not true!

The reality is the relationship of college majors to career fields varies. Some career choices dictate you choose a specific undergraduate major. However, most college majors don't offer specific preparation for a single type of work. The primary reason students choose the wrong major is that so many concentrate exclusively on studying for a specific "job," as if each job required a certain major. Your choice of a major is only one factor in determining your future job prospects and career path.

Key Questions:

- Who am I?
- What are my values?
- What am I passionate about?
- Who do I want to be?

Asking the Right Questions

Students often choose their majors unwisely because they lack sufficient information about themselves, potential courses of study, the job market, and how to combine education and career goals. This is why some self-exploration is necessary. Before you choose your major, you should be asking yourself some key questions.

Begin to chart your college career, using your career goals as the basis for decisions about your academic major and minor, elective courses, internships, vacation jobs, leadership commitments and extracurricular activities.

Strategies for Choosing A Major

One option is to major in something with a high potential for your human development. Another option is to consider a community college program that provides a good background for the professional areas you hope to enter in a four-year university.

There is always the option of following your passion and living your dream. Or, you can develop a marketable combination of liberal arts major with a practical coursework concentration which involves the use of manual or practical abilities.

For example, a student who has dreams of owning an exclusive upscale spa and salon may choose to major in business administration at a four-year university and combine that with licensure in cosmetology from a reputable cosmetology school.

Evaluating the Majors/Careers You are Considering

Keep in mind that, while researching and evaluating majors, you need to be realistic about what you will be required to do and what you are willing to commit to doing. In order to conduct a proper evaluation of possible majors, consider the following:

- How many credits/courses are needed in order to graduate in that major?
- How long will this take?
- What is the future outlook for this major?
- What else can you do with this major?
- What are graduates with this major doing now?

Going Beyond Your Major

Because job markets will be much more competitive when you finish your degree, you should think about going beyond your major.

- Develop skills that are immediately useful to the employer through leadership opportunities outside the classroom. Plan to gain additional experience through summer or part-time work, intern/externships, volunteer experience, extracurricular activities, and elective courses.

- Become competitive in today's market by obtaining the experience and competencies related to your chosen field.

- Avoid prematurely commiting to a field you don't yet understand, or concentrating on one area of knowledge that may lead to excluding other areas that have not yet been discovered.

Making Your Degree Marketable

- Make your degree marketable by choosing a school with a great reputation.

- Establish a strong career plan.

- Supplement your degree with work experience and elective coursework to support your career goals.

- Consider combining your liberal arts degree with solid technical skills.

Quick Tips

1. **Be truthful to yourself.**
   Now is the time to take a minute and ask yourself some deep personal questions about what you want out of your life and how college can help you achieve your goals. Remember to tell yourself the truth.

2. **Take advantage of the Career Development resources offered at your community college.**
   Check to see what types of programs or assessments you can take. Make an appointment with a career counselor to discuss your career options and what majors will be applicable to that career choice.

3. **Do research about the career and major you are considering.**
   What is the job outlook for this career? Do you know how long it takes to get the degree you need? Make sure you are well informed and willing to commit what it takes to accomplish this goal.

4. **Remember you do not have to be 100 percent certain of your major to choose your college but it does help.**
   Knowing your major will help you choose the right college and the right program. This can save you time and money in the long run.

Exercise 1.1: Your Dream Job

Your task for this activity is to think back to when you were a child. A time in your life when your imagination was vivid and bold. When you were excited about all of the great possibilities that existed for you. What was it you dreamed of becoming one day? What job did you want to have when you were a dreamer...before the realities and limitations of life changed your mind?

Think about your past dream jobs then, think about your current dream jobs. Do this without the influence of what is or is not realistic. Don't think about money, job security, how much education is required, or what people will think. Just think about your dreams.

What are your top three dream jobs?

1. [   ]
2. [   ]
3. [   ]

Choose two dream jobs listed to complete this exercise.

1. [   ]
2. [   ]

Are there similarities between the jobs you selected? What are they? If different, what draws you to two completely different jobs? Name the specific characteristics or elements that appealed to you.

[   ]

Are these jobs realistic for you? Why or why not? Are you willing to do what it takes to achieve this career at this point your life? Why or why not?

[   ]

Consider what types of jobs are more realistic for you that are related to these dream jobs. What are some of them?

[   ]

Think about what majors relate to your dream jobs. What are those majors and how do they relate?

[   ]

Exercise 1.2: Asking Yourself The Right Questions

This is your chance to really think about who you are and how you want the world to perceive you. Read the questions below carefully and think honestly about your responses to them. Record your responses in the spaces provided below. Remember, be honest.

1. Who am I?

2. What do I believe in?

3. What are my values?

4. Who do I want to be?

5. What do I really want out of my life?

6. What am I passionate about?

7. What am I good at? What skills do I have?

8. What goals have I set for myself?

9. Why did I come to college?

10. How do I want the world to perceive me?

11. What are my greatest fears?

12. What legacy do I want to leave behind?

Exercise 1.3: Evaluating Your Careers and Majors

The following worksheet will help you evaluate the best major for the career you plan to pursue.

Answer the following questions:

1. What is your chosen career?

2. What are the skills needed for this career?

3. What academic training is required for your career (bachelor's, master's, etc.)?

4. Is there any additional certification, licensing or credentialing required beyond a bachelor's degree? If so, what type?

5. How long will this take and are you willing to commit?

Visit www.myplan.com/majors or http://uncw.edu/career/WhatCanIDoWithaMajorIn.html

6. What will be your college major, concentration and/or minor for your career choice?

7. Describe this major.

8. What else can you do with this major? List and describe at least four career titles related to this major.

Chapter 1 Reflection: Beginning the Journey

Before you move on to the next chapter, take a moment to reflect on what you discovered in this chapter and how you can apply it to your goals.

1. What are the two most important things you learned in this chapter and how will you apply those things to your goal of transferring successfully to a four-year college or university?

2. What major did you choose?

3. How confident are you feeling about your decision?

4. What do you need to do next?

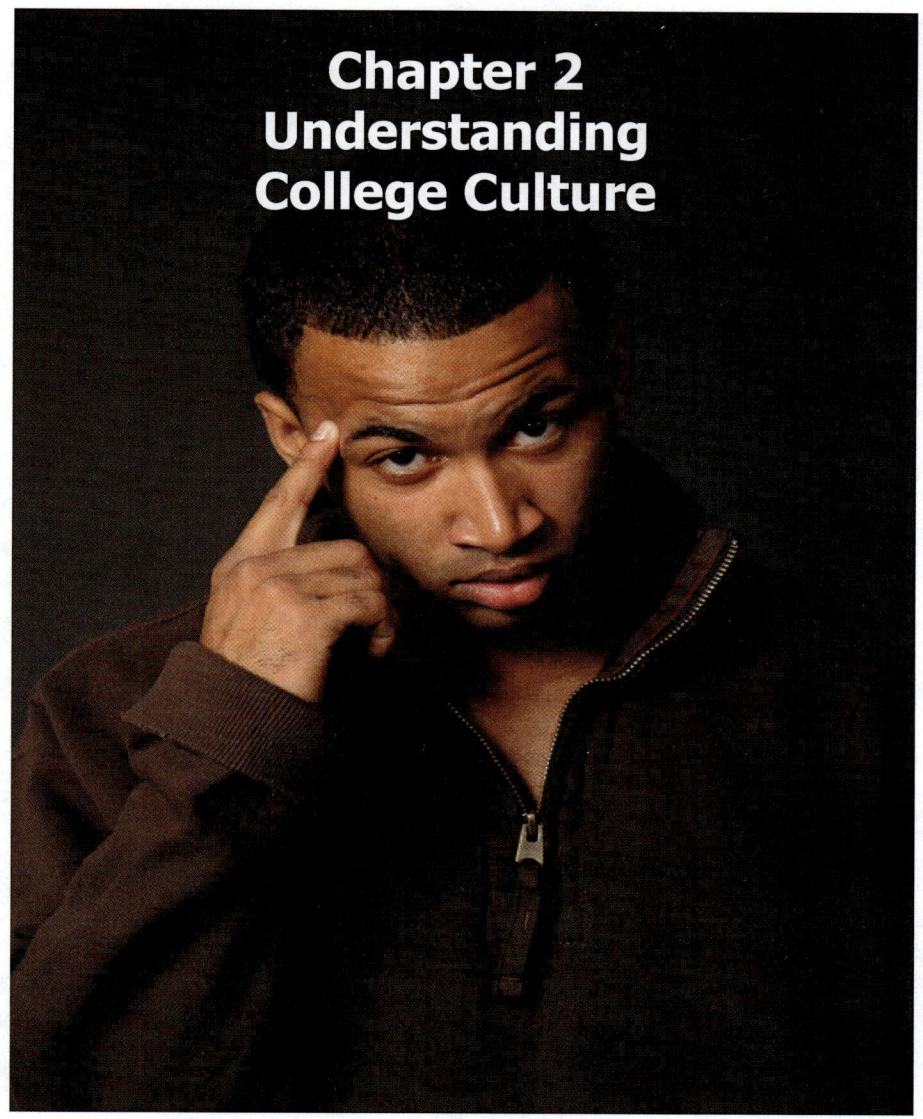

Chapter 2
Understanding
College Culture

"Most people spend more time and energy going around problems than in trying to solve them." — Henry Ford

In this chapter you will:

✔ Research Different Types of Colleges & Universities
✔ Explore Your Individual College Needs
✔ Investigate the Best Colleges for Your Career & Major

College Culture

So you have chosen your major and now you are ready to choose the four-year college or university that you will attend to continue your education. So many decisions and options are in front of you! Should you go to a school near your home? Should you go to a public or private university? Would you prefer a large or small campus? In this chapter you will review the decision making process, explore the different types of colleges in the United States and then select the top three colleges for you.

College culture can be described as the combination of academic focus, language, behavior, values, philosophy and outlook that are part of a college education. It is the unspoken "rules" that college students learn to fit into a college environment. College cultures differ depending on the campus, but there are some similarities.

The first thing you should know about college culture is the change in the learning culture. In the early 1970s, Malcolm Knowles introduced the United States to the concept that adults and children learn differently.

Pedagogy refers to the assumptions and strategies for teaching children. It literally means the art and science of teaching children. The theories and strategies that apply to adult learning are called andragogy which means the art and science of helping adults learn.

Pedagogy
- Applies to elementary and secondary education.
- The student's learning is teacher-directed learning.
- Student behavior is closely monitored / controlled.
- To be promoted, the learner only needs to know what the teacher deems relevant.

Andragogy
- This term applies to post-secondary education.
- Learning is student-directed.
- Learners need to know that what, how and why information is relevant to their life and goals.
- It is assumed that the student will be responsible.
- Student's life experiences become a part of the learning experience.

At the collegiate level, you become an adult learner. E. C. Lindeman had five key assumptions about adult learners.

1. Adults are motivated to learn as they experience needs and interests that learning will satisfy.
2. Adults' orientation to learning is life-centered.
3. The richest source for the adult's learning is experience.
4. Adults have a deep need to direct themselves.
5. People's individual differences increase with age.

(Knowles, Holton III, and Swanson, 2005)

The Different Types of Colleges in the United States

One of your current tasks is figuring out what college is the best fit for your individual, financial and career needs. In the spirit of andragogy you will be taking a close look at your personal needs and directing yourself in making decisions about which college environment you will choose to transfer to. Size, location, campus culture and cost are just a few of the factors to consider in making such a decision. Let's explore the different types of college environments that exist.

Community Colleges
- Two-year colleges offering associate degrees and certifications that focus on career readiness prepare you to continue getting an education or to enter the workforce immediately
- Often an affordable and convenient option

Examples: Central Piedmont Community College, Wake Tech Community College, Forsyth Tech Community College

Vocational-Technical & Career Colleges
- Offer specialized training to students who are interested in a particular industry or career
- Students not required to take general education classes in all subjects
- Offer certificates of completion or associate degrees

Examples: Paul Mitchell School of Cosmetology, Presbyterian School of Nursing

Liberal Arts Colleges
- Most are private and focus on undergraduates
- Typically offer four-year programs leading to a bachelor's degree
- Majors include literature, philosophy, history, languages, mathematics, humanities, and social and natural sciences
- First two years include general education courses, then students choose a major

Examples: Wingate University, Davidson College, High Point College

Universities
- Larger and offer more majors and degree options (BS/A, MS/A, Ph.D.)
- Most universities contain several smaller colleges
- May have to apply to a specific college within the university
- Can prepare for many types of careers or for further study in graduate school
- Can be public or private

Examples: Appalachian State University, East Carolina University

Ivy League
- Often viewed by the public as some of the most prestigious universities worldwide; consistently ranked among the top 15 universities in the U.S.
- Associated with academic excellence, selectivity in admissions, social elitism and large endowments

Examples: Brown University, Princeton University, University of Pennsylvania, Yale University

Arts Colleges
- Focus on the arts
- Provide training in, for example, photography, music, theater or fashion design
- Most usually offer associate or bachelor's degrees in fine arts or a specialized field

Examples: California College of the Arts, Art Institute, Savannah College of Art and Design

More Types of Colleges and Universities

As you can see there many options to choose from in considering which college is the best fit for your individual needs. The challenge is for you to be truthful about what your needs are, not what others believe is right for you or what the most popular choice might be. Statistics have shown that choosing the right college has a significant impact on your success as a student and your motivation to complete your degree.

Single Gender
- Specifically for men or for women
- Historically, many U.S. colleges were gender-segregated (until late 1860s)
- Liberal arts, private and the focus is on undergrad studies

Examples: Meredith College (Raleigh), Trinity University, Wellesley, Morehouse, Hampden Sydney

Religiously Affiliated
- Affiliated with a religious faith
- Usually private

Examples: Davidson College, St. Andrews Presbyterian College, University of Notre Dame

Special Interests
- Focus on a specific type of student population or area of interest

Examples: Gallaudet University (for the Deaf and hard of hearing), Military Institutions (Naval Academy, Virginia Military Institute)

Historically Black Colleges/Universities (HBCUS)
- Majority African American
- Programs, services and activities relevant to African-American students

Examples: Johnson C. Smith University, Winston-Salem State University

Hispanic Serving
- 25 percent full-time population is made up of Hispanic students

Examples: Arizona Western College, Valencia College (FL)

Online Colleges
- Majority of classes offered online
- Convenience of taking class from home
- May require more coursework to compensate for not physically attending the class in person

Examples: University of Phoenix, Capella University, Liberty University Online

Public Colleges/Universities
- Funded by local and state governments
- Lower tuition for in-state students

Examples: University of North Carolina Chapel Hill, North Carolina State University

Private Colleges/Universities
- Selective admission
- Funded by private sector
- Not administered by local, state or national government

Examples: Queens University of Charlotte, Wake Forest University

Making Decisions

As you work through these decisions, you will want to think about your decision making style and process. How have you made decisions in the past? Are you analytical or do you go with your "gut?" Do you overanalyze and get into analysis paralysis? Do you like to talk things over with many people in your life or sit and think quietly on your own?

Throughout your college experience and life, you will be confronted with the inevitable need to make decisions. This can be an overwhelming task that if not done properly, can have unfavorable results. There is a formal process to help you make effective decisions. The Decision Making Process is the cognitive process of choosing between alternative courses of action. Let's take a look at the steps!

> **Decision-making steps:**
> 1. Defining the issue
> 2. Investigating and analyzing the issue
> 3. Developing possible solutions
> 4. Selecting the best solution
> 5. Translating the decision into effective action

Step 1: Define and State the Real Issue

This is your opportunity to define and clarify the real issue. In order to do this properly you must first determine if you are dealing with the important or relevant aspects of an issue or if you are just focusing on the visible symptoms. Problems are often the symptom and not the true problem. For example, not getting the internship of your choice (symptom) may reflect not submitting a strong application (problem); your rejection for admission to your number one college choice (symptom) may be because you waited until the last minute to work on your applications or because you did not prepare for the SAT (problem).

Take time to think about what your issue is. This is not a matter for haste, but meant for careful inspection and deliberation. Start to determine conditions of the ideal solution and balance long range goals. You might even find it necessary to change traditional approaches.

Step 2: Investigate and Analyze the Issue

In this step you will identify specific elements contributing to the issue/problem that must be found and changed. Be sure that you gather all the facts and understand what they mean. Establish goals that solving the problem should accomplish and determine the requirements that the solution to the problem must meet. Ask yourself, what are the goals that resolving this issue should accomplish? This is also an opportunity to investigate and eliminate undesirable or unwise courses of action.

Step 3: Develop Possible Solutions

To begin this step, brainstorm possible options and solutions. Develop several alternative solutions for the issue and avoid "either-or" plans. This forces us to test the validity of our basic assumptions. It does not necessarily guarantee a right decision, but at least the problem has been thought through.

Remember that sometimes, to take no action at all may be one of the alternatives. This requires a decision too. However, it should not be done just to avoid something unpleasant.

Step 4: Determine the Best Solution

It is rare for an issue to have only one solution. The challenge is to select the best solution for you. Always make the best decision in light of the given facts. Consider using the technique of comparing the pros and cons of each option. This will help you think through and determine which solution seems to offer the best results with the least disturbance to your goals. Weigh your pros and cons by identifying the options or possible solutions. Then list the pros and cons for each of the possible solutions. Assign each pro and con a point value of one to five, with one being the least significant and five being the most significant. Finally, total the points in both columns. The column with the most points is your best option.

Remember, even the best solution has its risks and gains. Appraise the odds of each alternative. Also, be prepared to correct the decision if new information indicates a change in status. Some questions that you might ask yourself during this step are:

- What is the potential impact this decision will have?

- Will this solution serve long-term needs?

Step 5: Translate the Decision into Effective Action

Here is where you create a plan for your decision and realize it. Consider time a factor. You should be cognizant of deadlines and be sure that it can be accomplished in a realistic period of time. Be prepared to explain your decision to those involved and affected. And always follow up to both ensure proper and effective implementation and evaluate the effects of the decision that you made.

Quick Tips

Cast a wide net

It's perfectly okay to have a favorite or first choice for your transfer college, but choose at least five to seven other colleges to investigate as well. If you don't get into your first choice, it's always good to have a back-up plan. Don't make the mistake of only applying to your first choice and then missing out on other opportunities due to deadlines and unmet requirements.

1. **Be unafraid to apply to "fantasy" colleges.**

   You might also be surprised. Apply to at least three colleges which are unlikely to admit you. Also, be sure to choose "safety" schools you would be happy to attend. These may be considered "safety" schools due to their cost.

2. **Look into colleges that you know little or nothing about.**

   It's a good idea to research at least two or three colleges you know little or nothing about but offer the major that interests you. Read student reviews and news articles about the colleges you are considering. It is sometimes a good idea to look outside your comfort zone.

3. **Never choose a college based on where your friends go.**

   One of the worst reasons to choose a college is because your friends go there. You can plan to visit your friend during breaks and vacations.

4. **Never choose a college based on your favorite athletic team.**

   A great football team doesn't necessarily mean a great academic program. We like to follow the teams we grew up loving but your priority when choosing a college should be academic and career related. Don't equate educational quality with name recognition.

5. **Investigate for yourself.**

   Separate reality from baseless opinions. "Hard to get into," "A party school," or "Too expensive" for someone else doesn't necessarily ring true for you. Don't accept generalizations without evidence. Do your research.

6. **Don't rule out all colleges early because of cost.**

   Many colleges offer scholarships, financial aid, tuition installment plans and student work programs that make them far more affordable. Make sure you research all financial aid options and speak to a counselor so you are well prepared for deadlines and applications that need to be completed.

7. **Don't put all your eggs in one basket.**

   The College Board states that students should apply to five to eight institutions, including a range of safety schools (colleges students are positive they'll get into) to reach schools, where admissions may be more of a stretch for some students.

Exercise 2.1: Decision Making Worksheet

Think about what issues exist that are associated with your successful transfer to a senior college/university, then complete this worksheet based on one of those issues.

Step 1: Define and State Your Real Issue

[ ]

Step 2: Investigate and Analyze the Issue

What are the specific elements contributing to the issue?

[ ]

What are the facts related to this issue?

[ ]

What are your long-term goals related to this issue?

[ ]

What is the ideal outcome?

[ ]

Step 3: Develop Possible Solutions

What are two possible solutions?

Solution 1

[ ]

Solution 2

[ ]

Step 4: Determine the Best Solution

Complete the table below using the **two possible solutions in step 3.** Don't forget to weigh your pros and cons. To do this, use the tables below to identify the possible solutions, then list the pros and cons for the possible solution. Assign each pro and con a point value of one to five, with one being the least significant, and five being the most significant. Total the points in both columns, then subtract the total points for your cons from the total points for your pros to give you the total solution point value. The solution with the greatest point value is the best solution for your issue.

Table 1

Possible Solution 1:			
Pros (Advantages)	Points	Cons (Disadvantages)	Points
Total Points		Total Points	
Total Solution Point Value			

Table 2

Possible Solution 2:			
Pros (Advantages)	Points	Cons (Disadvantages)	Points
Total Points		Total Points	
Total Solution Point Value			

What is the best solution for your issue?

What is the potential impact this decision will have?

Will this solution serve your long-term needs?

Step 5: Translating the Decision into Effective Action

What is your action plan?

By what date will you complete your action plan?

What are four things that you can do this week in order to translate the decision into effective action?

1.

2.

3.

4.

Exercise 2.2: College Search Evaluation

In this exercise, you will analyze and determine what characteristics of a college/university are most appealing to your individual needs. This worksheet will help you discover the best college for you based on what you value and consider most important.

Table 1: For this first activity, use the table to list and rank the factors related to your personal college needs.

Factors	Rank
Cost	1.
Location	2.
Major & Concentration	3.
Campus Size	4.
Type of College Culture	5.
Housing Needs	6.
Campus Life	7.

Table 2: For this activity, consider what you have learned about college culture so far. Use the table below to help you decide what cultural factors of a college campus you prefer. Select one of the factors listed on each row.

Type of College Culture			
	Large University	Small College	
	Public	Private	
	Co-Ed	Single Gender	
	Traditional	Online/Evening	
	Big Metropolitan Location	Small Town Location	
	Ethnically Diverse	Minority Serving	
	In-state	Out-of-state	

Table 3: List three colleges would you consider attending. If you have less than three, then visit: www.mycollegeguide.org to get a generalized list of schools:

A: [   ]

B: [   ]

C: [   ]

Table 4: In the table below, enter your score on a scale of 0-5 (5 being the best fit and 0 being no fit) to judge each feature for each school. Consider each feature by asking yourself, "Am I comfortable with this feature of the school?," or "Do I like this feature of the school?" When evaluating factual information, such as "Is my major offered?," enter a 5 for yes and 0 for no.

Sample qualities:	College A	College B	College C
Is my major offered?			
Distance from home			
Campus size			
Ethnic make up			
Average # of years to graduate			
City/town size and makeup			
Cost			
Gender make up			
What do my instincts tell me?			
Personal Quality 1:			
Personal Quality 2:			
Personal Quality 3:			
Total School Value:			

Based on your finding, rank your top three college choices.

1. [   ]

2. [   ]

3. [   ]

Keep in mind that this exercise is to help guide you in the decision making process. It is not an absolute test in choosing which college you should attend.

Chapter 2 Reflection: College Culture

Before you move ahead to the next chapter, take a moment to reflect on what you discovered in this chapter and how you can apply it to your goal of transferring.

1. What are the two most important things you learned in this chapter and how will you apply those things to your goal of transferring successfully to a four-year college or university?

2. How did the results of the exercises compare to your expectations?

3. Are you confident in the choices you made? Were there any surprises or new college opportunities to consider?

4. What is the next step that you need to take?

**Chapter 3
Student Development**

"We must live what we want the world to become." — Gandhi

In this chapter you will:

✔ Explore Student Development and Support Services
✔ Learn About the Importance of Student Leadership and Civic Engagement

College Student Development & Student Affairs

Robert D. Brown, 50th President of the American College Personnel Association, said that cognitive and personal development on the collegiate level has been viewed as highly interlaced and that the whole student has been considered more than the educated parts. Student Affairs focuses on developing the whole student. It is the goal of promoting a marriage of the growth of intellectual development in the classroom and social development outside the classroom.

Student Affairs is a department or division of support services available to students at institutions of higher education. The programs and services are designed to enhance student growth and development for student success and degree completion. Student Affairs should work in collaboration with academic programs to provide opportunities for students to explore student life, health and wellness, leadership and service, civic engagement, and diversity.

The beginning of Student Affairs has been traced back to Athenian education and universities in The Middle Ages. In early American colleges, "in loco parentis," which means "in place of the parent," was the approach used to support students by acting as the parent while the student was attending college away from home. Through this approach, the focus was on control of the student, as opposed to the modern philosophy which focuses on the development of the student as a whole. (Delworth, Hanson and Associates, 1989)

By the end of the Civil War, in loco parentis was fading out and Student Services/Affairs began to emerge. The first Student Affairs professionals with a specific function were the Deans of Women and Men and personnel workers. Student Affairs is important to your development as a student because it can:

- Enhance student growth and development.
- Promote student success and degree completion.
- Ensure a richer college experience.
- Help students develop skills outside the classroom.

Depending on the college culture and climate, departments for Student Affairs will vary in service areas. Some of the more common areas include:

Academic and Support Services

- Academic Advising
    Helps students translate academic requirements established in the college course catalog into an academic plan specific to program and major
- Admissions
    Assists students with the processes and deadlines related to being admitted to the college/university
- Campus Ministries
    Provides spiritual guidance and comfort to students in need
- Campus Police/Security
    Provides a safe campus environment for college students, faculty and staff
- Career Services
    Guides and assists students with career development and workforce readiness

- Counseling Services
  - Offers support to students facing emotional challenges
- Disability Services
  - Works with all areas of the college to make sure that students with disabilities may independently meet the demands of college life
- Housing/Residence Life
  - Provides on-campus housing for students with programming that promotes personal, social, educational and cultural development
- New Student Orientation
  - Provides new students with programs and information necessary for a smooth transition and success in the college environment
- Multicultural Affairs
  - Promotes diversity and inclusion among college students, faculty and staff

Campus Life

- Greek (Fraternity & Sorority) Life
  - Is responsible for managing and advising the entire Greek community at the university
- Health & Wellness
  - Promotes and advocates students' physical, emotional and psychological health and awareness
- LGBTA (Lesbian, Gay, Bisexual Transgender Association)
  - Works to foster a safe inclusive college environment and to be an advocate for gender identity issues. Programs and services are designed to increase awareness and improve campus climates
- Recreation
  - Is responsible for club team sports usually sponsored by the Campus Intramural or Recreation department. Men's, women's, and co-ed (men & women) teams of all different skill levels compete in a variety of sports
- Student Activities & Programming
  - Provides campus-wide programs and events that promote educational, cultural and social development

Student Leadership and Civic Engagement

One of the most important aspects of student development is the growth that happens outside the classroom. Student leadership and civic engagement are arguably the most beneficial extracurricular activities a student can perform while in college. Student leadership is a learning environment that encourages hands-on experiential learning and development. Organizing and planning, critical thinking and problem solving, effective communication, and working with and leading teams are some of the portable leadership skills students build while engaged in leadership and civic responsibilities.

As a prospective transfer student, it is beneficial to note that senior colleges and universities look favorably upon students that demonstrate evidence of leadership and personal development during their college experience. Here are some ways you can get involved in leadership opportunities at your college:

Student Leadership and Civic Engagement

- Student Government Association (SGA)
- Clubs and Organizations
- Learning Communities
- Fraternities and Sororities
- Service Learning

The rich experience of student leadership and civic engagement will work well for you beyond college. The skills mentioned can easily be transferred into the professional arena once you complete your college experience. In fact, these are skills that companies find valuable in graduates they are considering for employment.

In his 2010 research on recruiting trends, Phil Gardner of Michigan State heard these statements from employers:

"If you're not working, you should be volunteering somewhere. Get involved and get noticed."
"Be involved on campus. A degree by itself even with a high GPA means very little. Community involvement, leadership, and past work experience are much more highly regarded when a recruiter reviews a résumé."

By becoming involved on your college campus in leadership and volunteer experiences you can build your skills and your résumé for your future.

Students who have participated in leadership and civic opportunities often find:

- they are better prepared for the workforce.
- they often become industry leaders.
- they have more career marketability.

For example, college students may worry because they do not always have the extensive work experience that employers are looking for when they attempt to seek employment. There are many ways to get experience that will gain the attention of hiring managers and recruiters. These include internships, co-ops, civic engagement, volunteer work, leadership, study abroad, or research with faculty. All of these are experiences that can build skills and competencies that will give you a competitive edge during the interview process.

What Skills Are Employers Looking For

Yes, you need to have a good GPA and relevant work experience, but your "soft skills" are also crucial when looking for a job.

When it comes to the importance of candidate skills/qualities, employers are looking for team players who can solve problems, organize their work, and communicate effectively, according to respondents to NACE's *Job Outlook 2014* survey. (NACE is the National Association of Colleges and Employers). The list of skills and qualities that employers wanted candidates to have are listed below in ranked order.

1. Ability to work in a team structure

2. Ability to make decisions and solve problems

3. Ability to plan, organize and prioritize work

4. Ability to verbally communicate with persons inside and outside the organization

5. Ability to obtain and process information

6. Ability to analyze quantitative data

7. Technical knowledge related to the job

8. Proficiency with computer-related programs

9. Ability to create or edit written reports

10. Ability to sell or influence others

Remember, much of your development as a person occurs outside the classroom. Take advantage of programs, opportunities and services offered at your college or in your community to develop your leadership and interpersonal skills. Doing so will not only be beneficial to your career, but also to your success as an individual.

Quick Tips

1. **Attend New/Transfer Student Orientation Programs.**
   As soon as you get to campus be sure to attend Transfer/New Student Orientation. This is how you will be introduced to the college services available to you. Also establish a relationship with Student Affairs.

2. **Evaluate your academic strengths and weaknesses.**
   Identify your academic weaknesses early so that you know the areas in which you might need help and locate the office that can help you.

3. **Identify your transferable skills.**
   College is a great place to build your skill set. Sharpen and improve these skills because they transition well from college life to the world of employment.

4. **Assess and embrace your leadership style.**
   Figure out what kind of leader you are so that you'll know how and where your talents can be best utilized.

5. **Reinvent yourself.**
   No matter what type of student you have been in the past, college is a great place to become a new you. If you were introverted, become more outgoing. If you were disorganized, become more focused. College is where you start to become the person you want the world to perceive you as.

Exercise 3.1: Assessing Your Transferable Skills Exercise

To help you determine which of the skills you already possess and which need to be improved or developed, take a moment to evaluate your aptitudes. Review the list of skills below.

If you had to rate yourself on a scale of 1-5 (5 being highest/1 being lowest), how would you rate yourself?

_____ Ability to work in a team structure

_____ Ability to make decisions and solve problems

_____ Ability to plan, organize and prioritize work

_____ Ability to verbally communicate with persons inside and outside the organization

_____ Ability to obtain and process information

_____ Ability to analyze quantitative data

_____ Technical knowledge related to the job

_____ Proficiency with computer related programs

_____ Ability to create or edit written reports

_____ Ability to sell or influence others

After rating your skills, what are your top 2-3 strengths?

1.
2.
3.

What are your top 2-3 areas for improvement?

1.
2.
3.

What are some leadership or volunteer opportunities you could participate in to gain more experience with these particular skills?

Leadership or Volunteer Opportunity	Skills
1.	
2.	
3.	

Exercise 3.2: Student Affairs

Visit the website of one of the senior colleges/universities that you are interested in transferring to. Once on the website, find the Web page for the Student Affairs Division and complete this worksheet.

Name of College/University: _____

1. How does the college define it's Student Affairs division and what is the mission of the university's Student Affairs department?

2. What is the student activity fee at this university and what does this fee cover?

3. List three academic and three social challenges that you might face at a four-year college.

4. In which areas of Student Affairs would you find assistance overcoming each of these challenges?

Chapter 3 Reflection: Student Development

Before you move on to the next chapter, take a moment to reflect on what you discovered in this chapter and how you can apply it to your goals.

1. What are the two most important things you learned in this chapter and how will you apply those things to your goal of transferring successfully to a four-year college or university?

2. What did you learn about yourself from the transferable skills assessment?

3. Do you feel more comfortable now that you know the support services available to you? Why or why not?

4. What action steps do you need to take next?

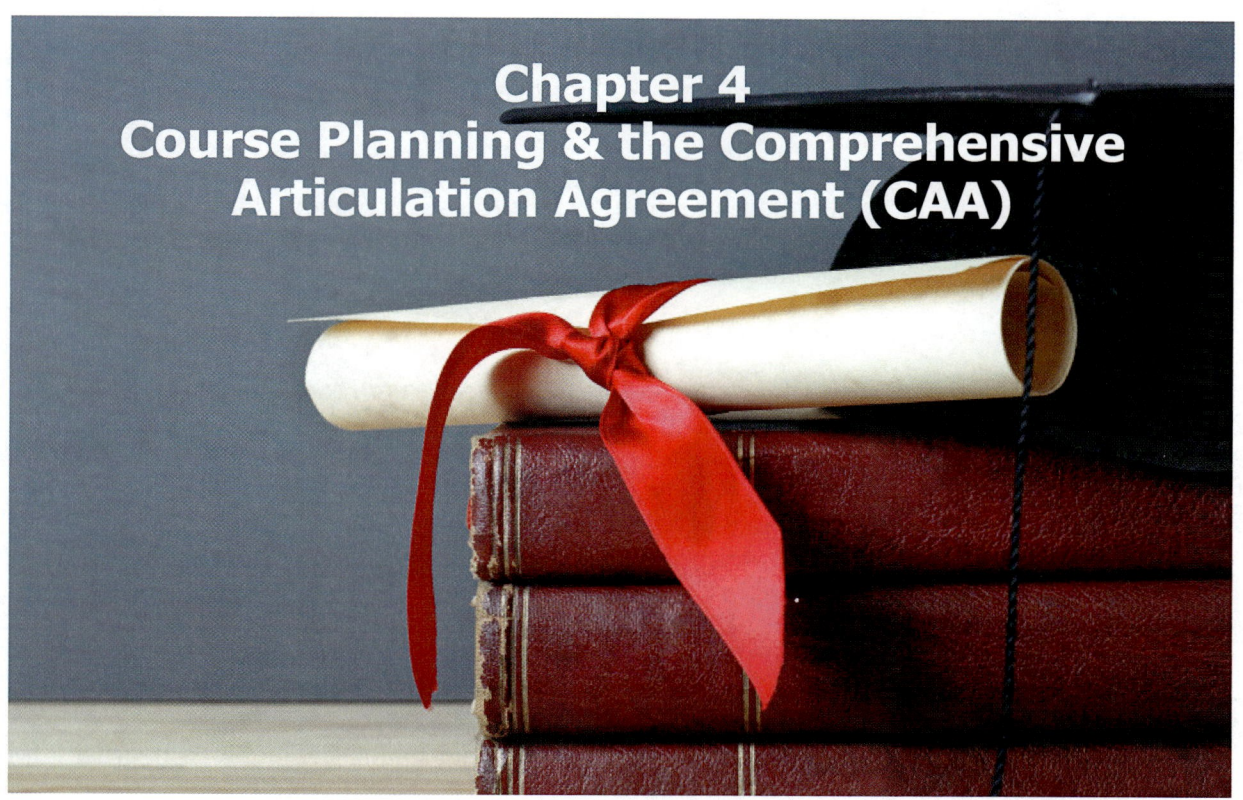

**Chapter 4
Course Planning & the Comprehensive
Articulation Agreement (CAA)**

"Go confidently in the direction of your dreams. Live the life you have imagined."
— Henry David Thoreau

In this chapter you will:

✔ **Investigate Degree Requirements**
✔ **Learn About Course Planning and the CAA**
✔ **Complete Your Academic Plan and Degree Checklist**

Course Planning and the Comprehensive Articulation Agreement (CAA)

In previous chapters you researched the educational requirements for your career and selected the major that will best prepare you for that career. Now it's time to take a realistic look at pursuing the course requirements for a degree in your chosen major.

One of the most significant things you will learn during this course is the importance of course planning and progression to your successful transfer to a four-year college. Course planning and progression refers to the sequence of course work a student must take in order to satisfy the academic requirements of an intended degree.

Course planning is important because:

- it provides a clear view of the academic requirements needed to receive a degree.
- it helps you establish academic goals with a realistic date for completion.
- it allows one to evenly balance out the course workload each semester.

The concept of successful course planning is dependent on many things. Some of the most vital are being discussed in this chapter. In fact, there are three important steps to successful course planning.

Step 1   **Know what academic training and credentialing is required for your career field. This includes understanding:**

- how course requirements relate to and vary based on your major and intended degree.
- what major or degree program will best prepare you for a career in that field.
- which courses you must take to fulfill the requirements for that major.
- the different levels of college degrees (see table below).

Table 1

Type of Degree	Description	Common Majors	Admissions Requirements
Certification	A designation earned by a person to assure qualification to perform a job or task.	Certified Public Accountant, Licensed Personal Counselor, Registered Nurse, Teaching, Handyman Welding	Dependent on degree earned, exam scores, and experience
Associates (AA, AS, AFA)	Consists of general education courses and usually takes two years to complete. Majors vary depending on program interests.	Arts, Fine Arts, Science, Graphic Design, Welding, HVAC, Nursing	May have open admissions; High School Diploma required
Bachelors (BA, BS)	Undergraduate studies. Four-year degree considered the entry level degree for several fields and will have academic major attached to it.	Business, English, Biology, Chemistry, Sociology, Pre –law, Engineering, Education, Pre-med	Dependent on school and major; GPA, Scholastic Assessment Test (SAT) score

(Table 1 Cont.)

Masters (MA, MS, MBA)	Granted to individuals who have undergone study demonstrating a mastery or high-order overview of a specific field of study or area of professional practice. Post undergraduate level course work. Usually takes two or three years to complete.	Counseling, Social Work, Business, Psychology, Student Affairs for Higher Ed	Dependent on bachelor's major, GPA, Graduate Record Examinations (GRE) scores, and Master's program
Doctorate of Philosophy (PhD)	Usually based on at least three years graduate study and a dissertation; the highest collegiate degree obtainable.	History, Higher Ed Administration, Mathematics, Biology	Dependent on bachelor's major, GPA, Graduate Record Examinations (GRE) scores, and Ph.D. program

Step 2 Understand what a college course catalog is and how to use it. This includes:

- being knowledgeable of the jargon.
- understanding how to read and comprehend course descriptions.

Keeping up with the academic terminology on the collegiate level can be challenging. Below is a list of some of the jargon you will hear throughout your college experience. It is also important to note that these terms may be different in other states.

Table 2

The Jargon/Terms You Should Know

Major: The area of academic study in which the student focuses or concentrates. There are required courses that must be taken in order to receive a degree in a major.

Major Concentration: A focus within a major. For example, a student might choose to major in Business Administration with a finance concentration.

Minor: The secondary field of study. It must be different from the major and it requires the student to take fewer credits. Some universities have requirements for acceptance into the minor program.

Transferable Courses: College-level courses that will transfer to a four-year college or university. Depending on the course and the four-year college's course requirements, transferable courses may or may not fulfill the general course requirements. This means that the course may only count as an elective toward your major.

General Education Courses: The basic courses required for a four-year degree. These courses usually include some English, math, science, humanities and foreign languages. The number of credits required for each of these will vary depending on the college.

Elective Courses: Courses that will count as elective credits toward graduation at a four-year college. These courses are not required for a major, but can support another area related to your major.

(Table 2 Cont.)

Your Full- or Part-Time Course Load: This refers to the number of credit hours a student takes during a semester. Your full- or part-time status as a student directly affects the number of years it may take you to complete your degree. The number of credits required for part- or full-time status varies depending on the college. A full-time college course load is usually nine to eighteen credit hours.

Open Major: A common major at the college/university in which a student is automatically admitted into upon admittance to the university. Some common majors include English, history and political science.

Closed Major: Students must apply for acceptance into the intended major in addition to general admission to the university. Applying to the major program usually involves adhering to additional academic requirements as well.

Terminal Degree: The highest degree obtainable for a major.

Pre-Professional Programs: Careers that require a post undergraduate degree. Examples include law, medicine, dentistry, etc.

The Comprehensive Articulation Agreement

An agreement between the Community College system and the University of North Carolina system through which selected courses taught at a community college will be accepted by universities in the University of North Carolina system. For example, upon successful completion of ENG111, regardless of which community college teaches it, the credits will be accepted at all North Carolina state universities. In some states, this agreement may be referred to as Articulation Agreement or Transfer Agreement.

Universal General Education Transfer Component (UGETC)

The courses that transfer for lower division general education equivalency as part of the new CAA. The UGETC comprises a minimum of 30 semester hours of credit.

Example of a description in the college course catalog with the articulation agreement clause:

ENG 111. Expository Writing. 3.0 Credits. Class-3.0. Clinical-0.0. Lab-0.0. Work-0.0

This course is the required first course in a series of two designed to develop the ability to produce clear expository prose. Emphasis is placed on the writing process including audience analysis, topic selection, thesis support and development, editing, and revision. Upon completion, students should be able to produce unified, coherent, well-developed essays using standard written English. ***This course has been approved to satisfy the comprehensive articulation agreement Universal General Education Transfer Component (UGETC) in English composition.***

Step 3   Know and understand the course requirements for the colleges you are interested in transferring to and the correlation to the general education requirements at your community college.

This includes knowing:

- what type of degree you are pursuing.
- what transfer degree you should be enrolled in at the community college in order to transfer to a four-year college/university.
- how the comprehensive articulation agreement works between your community college and your four-year university.
- what general education classes you need to take while at the community college.
- how many credit hours are required for graduation with an associate or bachelor's degree.
- if your major at a four-year college is open or closed.
- in which area of the college/university your major is housed.
- what is the terminal degree for your major.

Knowing the course requirements for your intended degree will help you plan out the courses you need to be taking at a community college which will transfer to the four-year college of your choice. The first step to making sure that you are on the right path is to be enrolled in a college transfer associate degree. This degree is designed for students who plan to transfer to four-year colleges and universities and fulfills general education requirements. Transfer degrees include Associate in Arts and Associate in Science. The degree you choose should be determined by your intended major at the university.

> **Transfer Degree Majors**
> - **Associate in Arts: Education:** Business, English, History, Liberal Arts (College courses comprising the arts, humanities, and natural and social sciences)
> - **Associate in Science:** Engineering, Pre-Medicine, Biology, Chemistry, Math

There are many benefits to graduating with an associate degree from a North Carolina community college. They include:

- The CAA enables North Carolina community college graduates of two-year Associate in Arts (AA) and Associate in Science (AS) degree programs who are admitted to constituent institutions of The University of North Carolina to transfer with junior status.

- Universities cannot place requirements on students transferring under the CAA that are not required of their native students.
- A student who completes the Associate in Arts or Associate in Science degree prior to transfer to a UNC institution will have fulfilled the UNC institution's lower-division general education requirements.

- Due to degree requirements in some majors, additional courses at the UNC institution may be required beyond the general education courses and pre-major courses taken at the community college.

- Community college graduates of the Associate in Arts or Associate in Science degree programs who have earned 60 semester hours in approved transfer courses with a grade of "C" or better and an overall GPA of at least 2.0 on a 4.0 scale will receive at least 60 semester hours of academic credit upon admission to a UNC institution.

- Requirements for admission to some major programs may require additional pre-specialty courses beyond the pre-major taken at the community college. Students entering such programs may need more than two academic years of course work to complete the baccalaureate degree, depending on requirements of the program.

- All courses approved for transfer in the CAA are designated as fulfilling general education or pre-major/elective requirements (see Appendix G). While general education and pre-major courses may also be used as electives, elective courses may not be used to fulfill general education requirements.

- CAA courses taken beyond the 60-61 SHC of credit in which the student received less than a "C" will not negate the provisions of the CAA.

  (2014 Comprehensive Articulation Agreement between The University of North Carolina and The North Carolina Community College System)

Although it is beneficial to complete a degree before transferring, it is not required. You can complete as few as 24 transferable hours at a North Carolina community college and be eligible for transfer admission at a university. If you are not enrolled in an associate program, you should meet with an academic advisor, faculty advisor or guidance counselor to discuss your transfer options in more detail.

The 2014 Comprehensive Articulation Agreement (CAA)

The Comprehensive Articulation Agreement (CAA) applies to all 58 North Carolina community colleges and all 16 constituent institutions of The University of North Carolina. The CAA is applicable to all North Carolina community college students who successfully complete a course designated as transferable or graduate with an AA or AS degree and transfer to a constituent institution of The University of North Carolina. The regulations for implementation of the CAA were originally approved by the Board of Governors and the State Board of Community Colleges. The Transfer Advisory Committee (TAC) oversees refinements of the regulations and minor changes. Significant changes will be brought to the Board of Governors and the State Board of Community Colleges for review at the discretion of the respective Presidents of The University of North Carolina and the North Carolina Community College System.

The 2013 revision of CAA policies and curricula is designed to better facilitate the original purpose of the CAA to optimize the transfer of credits between the institutions of the North Carolina Community College System and the University of North Carolina institutions. The focus of the current review of the CAA includes:

1. supporting current general education requirements at senior institutions.
2. establishing a process for maintaining currency.
3. ensuring current information is universally accessible to students and advisors at both senior institutions and community colleges.

The revised Comprehensive Articulation Agreement serves as a current and adaptive agreement that supports more students completing both an associate or baccalaureate degree.

To be eligible for the transfer of credits under the CAA, the student must graduate from the community college with an Associate in Arts (AA) or Associate in Science (AS) degree and have an overall Grade Point Average (GPA) of at least 2.0 on a 4.0 scale and a grade of "C" or better in all CAA courses. Students who do not complete the degree are eligible to transfer credits on a course-by-course basis.

Transfer Assured Admissions Policy (TAAP)

The TAAP assures admission to one of the 16 UNC institutions under the following conditions:

- Admission is not assured to a specific campus or specific program or major.
- Students must have graduated from a North Carolina community college with an Associate in Arts or Associate in Science degree.
- Students must meet all requirements of the CAA.
- Students must have an overall GPA of at least 2.0 on a 4.0 scale, as calculated by the college from which they graduated, and a grade of "C" or better in all CAA courses.
- Students must be academically eligible for re-admission to the last institution attended.
- Students must meet judicial requirements of the institution to which they apply. Students must meet all application requirements at the receiving institution, including the submission of all required documentation by stated deadlines.

If a student is denied admission to a UNC institution, then he or she will be notified in writing by the institution. In this notification, the student will be directed to the College Foundation of North Carolina (CFNC) website (www.cfnc.org) where the student will be given information regarding space availability and contacts in the respective UNC Admissions offices. It is the student's responsibility to contact each institution's admissions office to get specific information about admissions and available majors.

If the previous steps do not result in admission to a UNC institution, then the student should contact the CFNC Resource Center at 1.866.866.CFNC.

Transfer Credit Appeal

If a transfer student perceives that the terms of the CAA have not been honored, he or she may follow the Transfer Credit Appeal Procedure. Each UNC and community college institution will provide a link to the Transfer Credit Appeal Procedure on its website.

Eligibility

To be eligible for the transfer of credits under the CAA, the student must graduate from the community college with an Associate in Arts (AA) or Associate in Science (AS) degree and have an overall Grade Point Average (GPA) of at least 2.0 on a 4.0 scale and a grade of "C" or better in all CAA courses. Students who do not complete the degree are eligible to transfer credits on a course-by course basis.

General Education Courses and Pre-major Courses

The Associate in Arts (AA) and Associate in Science (AS) degree programs in the North Carolina Community College System require a total of 60 or 61 semester hours credit for graduation and are transferable to any UNC institution. The overall total is comprised of both lower-division general education and pre-major courses. This curriculum reflects the distribution of discipline areas commonly included in institution-wide, lower-division general education requirements for the baccalaureate degree.

The Associate in Arts (AA) and Associate in Science (AS) degree programs include general education requirements that represent the fundamental foundation for success and include study in the areas of English composition, communications, humanities and fine arts, natural sciences and mathematics, and social and behavioral sciences. Within these discipline areas, community colleges must include opportunities for the achievement of competence in reading, writing, oral communication, fundamental mathematical skills, and basic computer use. Students must meet the receiving university's foreign language and/or health and physical education requirements, if applicable, prior to or after transfer to the senior institution.

The AA and AS degree programs of study are structured to include two components:

1. **Universal General Education Transfer Components** are the courses that transfer for lower division general education equivalency as part of the new CAA and comprises a minimum of 30 semester hours of credit.

2. **Additional general education, pre-major, and elective courses** which prepare students for successful transfer into selected majors at UNC institutions and bring the total number of hours in the degree programs to 60-61 semester hours.

Transfer of courses taken in other associate degree programs

Upon admission to another public two-year institution or to a public university, a community college student who was enrolled in an Associate in Applied Science (AAS) or Associate in Fine Arts (AFA) degree program and who satisfactorily completed the courses with a grade of "C" or better in all courses that are designated for college transfer (see Appendix G, CAA Transfer Course List) will receive credit for those courses. AAS or AFA students completing courses designated Universal General Education Transfer Component will receive equivalent general education course credit for those courses at the receiving institution. For courses not designated as Universal General Education Transfer Component, the receiving institution will determine whether the course will count as general education or pre-major/elective credit. Students in these programs who transfer must meet the general education requirements of the receiving institution.

Articulation of Associate in Fine Arts or Associate in Applied Science degree programs may be handled on a bilateral articulation agreement basis rather than on a state-wide basis. Under bilateral agreements, individual universities and one or more community colleges may join in a collaborative effort to facilitate the transfer of students from AFA or AAS degree programs to baccalaureate degree programs.

The TAC encourages the development of new bi-lateral articulation agreements among institutions; however, TAC will not maintain a current inventory of bilateral articulation agreements for AAS degree programs.

Transfer of courses not originated at North Carolina community colleges

Transfer courses that do not originate at a North Carolina community college or UNC institution may be used under the CAA with the following stipulations:

- Courses must be completed at a regionally accredited (e.g., SACS) institution of higher education.

- Courses must meet general education requirements.

- Courses may total no more than 14 semester hours of general education course credit.

- For courses not originating at a NC community college, if the courses are used to complete the AA or AS, the courses will transfer as part of the degree. Otherwise, if 14 hours or less are presented without completion of the AA or AS, then the receiving institution will consider the courses on a course-by-course basis.

The New 2014 CAA
60-61 Semester Hours of Credit (SHC) for Transfer Degree

45 SHC General Education
    • **31-34 Semester Hours of Universal General Education Transfer Component (UGETC), plus**
    • **11-14 additional Semester Hours of General Education courses selected from the Transfer Course list**

15 Semester Hours of Pre-Major Courses

New Curriculum	
Associate in Arts	**Associate in Science**
• English - 6 (SHC)	• English - 6 (SHC)
• Humanities/Arts – 9 (SHC)	• Humanities/Arts – 6 (SHC)
• Social/Behavioral Science – 9 (SHC)	• Social/Behavioral Science – 6 (SHC)
• Mathematics – 3-4 (SHC)	• Mathematics – 8 (SHC)
• Natural Science – 4 (SHC)	• Natural Science – 8 (SHC)
• Additional GEC – 13-14 (SHC)	• Additional GEC – 11 (SHC)
• Other Required Hours – 14 (SHC)	• Other Required Hours – 14 (SHC)
• ACA 122 – 1 (SHC)	• ACA 122 – 1 (SHC)

For a complete copy of the 2014 Comprehensive Articulation Agreement between The University of North Carolina and The North Carolina Community College System visit: www.nccommunitycolleges.edu/programs/comprehensive_a_a.htm

Comprehensive Articulation Agreement
Transfer Credit Appeal Procedure

University of North Carolina/North Carolina Community College System

Guiding Principle: If a student from a North Carolina Community College System (NCCCS) college believes the terms of the Comprehensive Articulation Agreement (CAA) have not been honored by a University of North Carolina (UNC) institution to which the student has been admitted, the student may invoke the CAA Transfer Credit Appeal Procedure.

Steps in Filing an Appeal

Step 1

- **By the last day of classes of the first semester for which admission is offered,** the student must submit a CAA Transfer Credit Appeal Form along with any supporting documentation to the director of admission at the UNC campus to which the student has been admitted. Students first enrolling at the senior institution in a summer session must submit their appeal by the end of the subsequent fall semester.

- **The student must specify on the appeal form the specific CAA language that is in contention. Appeals that lack this information will not be considered.**

- The Director of Admission will review the appeal and respond in writing (email or letter) to the student within 15 business days.

Step 2

- If the student is not satisfied with the decision of the Director of Admission, he/she may appeal on the same form to the **Chief Academic Officer (Provost)** of the University within 15 days of written notice of the director's decision.

- The Provost will review the appeal and respond in writing (email or letter) to the student within 15 business days of receiving the student's appeal.

Step 3

- If the student is not satisfied with the decision of the Provost, he/she may appeal to the Transfer Advisory Committee (TAC) subcommittee, composed of the co-chairs, a representative from the UNC General Administration, and a representative from the NCCCS. The student must submit the appeal to the subcommittee within 15 days of the receipt of the Provost's decision. The appeal to the TAC subcommittee should be sent to:

  UNC-GA Transfer Advisory Committee Member
  CAA Appeal, PO Box 2688, Chapel Hill, NC 27515

If a consensus is reached by the subcommittee, the student will be notified within 15 business days; if a consensus resolution is not reached, the appeal will be forwarded by the subcommittee to the full TAC within 10 business days. The TAC will review the appeal and notify the student of the final decision within 10 business days of receiving the appeal.

Comprehensive Articulation Agreement

Transfer Credit Appeal Procedure

University of North Carolina/North Carolina Community College System

Section 1: Student Information *(to be completed by the student submitting the form)*

- The completed form and any supporting documentation **must be submitted to the UNC institution's Director of Admission by the last day of classes of the first semester for which admission is offered.**

- You must specify the nature of the appeal and cite the specific CAA language that is in contention. Appeals that do not include this information cannot be considered.

Last Name: _____ First: _____ MI: _____
          (Please print or type)

Address: _____
        (Number and Street)   (City)   (State)   (Zip)

Telephone: _____ Email: _____
       (Area code/Number)

Last NC Community College Attended: _____

UNC institution offering admission: _____ beginning (semester/yr) _____

Section 2: Basis for your appeal

- State your concern(s), citing specific language in the CAA that is applicable to your contention. Attach supporting documents.

- The CAA may be found at the North Carolina Community Colleges System website: www.nccommunitycolleges.edu/Programs/comprehensive_a_a.htm .

Student Signature: _____ Date: _____

Quick Tips

1. **Plan early and identify requirements.**
   Learn the academic requirements for your major early and plan accordingly.

2. **Know required credentialing.**
   Know any credential requirements for your field beyond the degree for your major and make them a part of your plan.

3. **Talk to people working in the field.**
   Talk to professionals in your intended career field and find out what they majored in and seek any advice that might better prepare you.

4. **Always familiarize yourself with the course catalog.**
   Know the course descriptions at your community college and your four-year university.

5. **Know your subject strengths.**
   Are you strong in math and science or writing intensive subjects? Try to match your strengths with subjects required for your major.

6. **Balance out your academic schedules.**
   Spread your difficult subjects evenly throughout your college career to help balance out heavy course loads.

7. **Establish a relationship with a counselor.**
   Getting to know a counselor or professional at the school to which you wish to transfer can go a long way.

8. **Know how to calculate your GPA and what it means to be in good academic standing.**
   For example, in some colleges you must maintain a 2.0 GPA on a 4.0 scale to remain in good academic standing and to keep your financial aid intact. Find out more about these policies at your college.

Exercise 4.1: Academic Program Evaluation

Now that you have selected your major and minor, you will begin to investigate the academic requirements to graduate with a bachelor's degree in that major. To complete this assignment, go to the website of your first choice prospective transfer college/university. Find the program/major that you will pursue and answer the following questions.

Name of University: _____

1. List your intended major.

2. Does this university offer a degree for this major (concentration and/or minor)? What is the type of degree (BA, BS, etc.)?

3. Where is this major housed at the university (department, college of, etc.)?

4. Is this major open or closed? If closed, what are the special academic requirements   for admission to the program?

5. What is the total number of credit hours you have to complete in order to graduate with a bachelor's degree in this major from this university?

6. How many of the total hours must be taken in the major?

7. What transfer degree should you be enrolled in to transfer to this university for this major?

8. Complete the Degree Check List and the Academic Plan to find out what general education classes do you need to take while at the community college.

Exercise 4.2: Associate in Arts (A10100)

Curriculum Standard

Name: _____ Student ID#: _____

Advisor: _____ Graduation Semester: _____

The Associate in Arts degree shall be granted for a planned program of study consisting of a minimum of 60 semester hours of credit (SHC) of college transfer courses. Within the degree program, the institution shall include opportunities for the achievement of competence in reading, writing, oral communication, fundamental mathematical skills, and basic computer use.

Courses are approved for transfer through the Comprehensive Articulation Agreement (CAA). The CAA enables North Carolina community college graduates of two-year associate in arts programs who are admitted to constituent institutions of The University of North Carolina to transfer with junior status.

Community college graduates must obtain a grade of "C" or better in each course and an overall GPA of at least 2.0 on a 4.0 scale in order to transfer with a junior status. Courses may also transfer through bilateral agreements between institutions.

General Education (45 SHC)

The general education common course pathway includes study in the areas of English composition, humanities and fine arts, social and behavioral sciences, natural sciences and mathematics.

	Credits Taken	Credits Needed	Semester/ Year
Universal General Education Transfer Component *(All Universal General Education Transfer Component courses will transfer for equivalency credit.)* **English Composition (6 SHC)** *The following two English composition courses are required.* ENG 111 Writing & Inquiry (3 SHC) ENG 112 Writing/Research in the Disciplines (3 SHC)			

	Credits Taken	Credits Needed	Semester/ Year

Select three courses from the following, from at least two different disciplines **(9 SHC)**
 	
Communications
  COM 231   Public Speaking   (3 SHC)
 	
Humanities/Fine Arts
  ART 111   Art Appreciation   (3 SHC)
  ART 114   Art History Survey I   (3 SHC)
  ART 115   Art History Survey II   (3 SHC)
  ENG 231   American Literature I   (3 SHC)
  ENG 232   American Literature II   (3 SHC)
  MUS 110   Music Appreciation   (3 SHC)
  MUS 112   Introduction to Jazz   (3 SHC)
  PHI 215   Philosophical Issues   (3 SHC)
  PHI 240 Introduction to Ethics (3 SHC)			

Select three courses from the following, from at least two different disciplines:
 	
Social/Behavioral Sciences (9 SCH)
  ECO 251   Principles of Microeconomics   (3 SHC)
  ECO 252   Principles of Macroeconomics   (3 SHC)
  HIS 111   World Civilizations I   (3 SHC)
  HIS 112   World Civilizations II   (3 SHC)
  HIS 131   American History I   (3 SHC)
  HIS 132   American History II   (3 SHC)
  POL 120   American Government   (3 SHC)
  PSY 150   General Psychology   (3 SHC)
  SOC 210 Introduction to Sociology (3 SHC)			

Math (3-4 SHC)
Select one course from the following:
  MAT 143   Quantitative Literacy   (3 SHC)
  MAT 152   Statistical Methods I   (4 SHC)
  MAT 171 Pre-calculus Algebra (4 SHC)			

Natural Sciences (4 SHC)
Select four SHC from the following course(s):
  AST 111   Descriptive Astronomy   (3 SHC)
       and AST 111-A Descriptive Astronomy Lab (1 SHC)
  AST 151   General Astronomy I   (3 SHC)
       and AST 151-A General Astronomy Lab I   (1 SHC)
  BIO 110 Principles of Biology (4 SHC)			

cont'd	Credits Taken	Credits Needed	Semester/ Year
Natural Sciences (4 SHC) BIO 110 — Principles of Biology — (4 SHC) BIO 111 — General Biology I — (4 SHC) CHM 151 — General Chemistry I — (4 SHC) GEL 111 — Introductory Geology — (4 SHC) PHY 110 — Conceptual Physics — (3 SHC) and PHY 110-A Conceptual Physics Lab — (1 SHC) **Additional General Education Hours (13-14 SHC)** An additional 13-14 SHC of courses should be selected from courses classified as general education within the Comprehensive Articulation Agreement. Students should select these courses based on their intended major and transfer university. **Total General Education Hours Required: 45**			

Other Required Hours (15 SHC)
  Academic Transition (1 SHC)
   The following Course is Required:
    ACA 122 College Transfer Success — (1 SHC)
 	
An additional 14 SHC of courses should be selected from courses classified as pre-major, elective or general education courses within the CAA. Students should select those courses based on their intended major and transfer university.			

* One semester hour of credit may be included in a 61 SHC associate in arts program of study. The transfer of this hour is not guaranteed.			
Total Semester Hours Credit (SHC) in Program: 60-61*			

Students must meet the receiving university's foreign language and/or health and physical education requirements, if applicable, prior to or after transfer to the senior institution.

Associate in Arts Academic Plan

Semester 1 _____

Course Requirement	Credits	Grade
Total Credit Hours This Semester:		

Semester 2 _____

Course Requirement	Credits	Grade
Total Credit Hours This Semester:		

Semester 3 _____

Course Requirement	Credits	Grade
Total Credit Hours This Semester:		

Semester 4 _____

Course Requirement	Credits	Grade
Total Credit Hours This Semester:		

What is your projected date of completion? _____

Exercise 4.2: Associate in Science (A10400)

Curriculum Standard

Name: _____ Student ID#: _____

Advisor: _____ Graduation Semester: _____

The Associate in Science degree shall be granted for a planned program of study consisting of a minimum of 60 semester hours of credit (SHC) of college transfer courses. Within the degree program, the institution shall include opportunities for the achievement of competence in reading, writing, oral communication, fundamental mathematical skills, and the basic computer use.

Courses are approved for transfer through the Comprehensive Articulation Agreement (CAA). The CAA enables North Carolina community college graduates of two-year associate in science programs who are admitted to constituent institutions of The University of North Carolina to transfer with junior status.

Community college graduates must obtain a grade of "C" or better in each course and an overall GPA of at least 2.0 on a 4.0 scale in order to transfer with a junior status. Courses may also transfer through bilateral agreements between institutions.

GENERAL EDUCATION (45 SHC)

The general education common course pathway includes study in the areas of English composition, humanities and fine arts, social and behavioral sciences, natural sciences and mathematics.

	Credits Taken	Credits Needed	Semester/ Year
Universal General Education Transfer Component *(All Universal General Education Transfer Component courses will transfer for equivalency credit.)* **English Composition (6 SHC)** *The following two English composition courses are required.* ENG 111 Writing & Inquiry (3 SHC) ENG 112 Writing/Research in the Disciplines (3 SHC)			

	Credits Taken	Credits Needed	Semester/ Year
Select two courses from the following, from at least two different disciplines **(6 SHC)**			
Communications			
COM 231 Public Speaking (3 SHC)			
Humanities/Fine Arts			
ART 111 Art Appreciation (3 SHC)			
ART 114 Art History Survey I (3 SHC)			
ART 115 Art History Survey II (3 SHC)			
ENG 231 American Literature I (3 SHC)			
ENG 232 American Literature II (3 SHC)			
Humanities/Fine Arts *continued*			
MUS 110 Music Appreciation (3 SHC)			
MUS 112 Introduction to Jazz (3 SHC)			
PHI 215 Philosophical Issues (3 SHC)			
PHI 240 Introduction to Ethics (3 SHC)			
Social/Behavioral Sciences (6 SHC)			
Select two courses from the following, from at least two different disciplines:			
ECO 251 Principles of Microeconomics (3 SHC)			
ECO 252 Principles of Macroeconomics (3 SHC)			
HIS 111 World Civilizations I (3 SHC)			
HIS 112 World Civilizations II (3 SHC)			
HIS 131 American History I (3 SHC)			
HIS 132 American History II (3 SHC)			
POL 120 American Government (3 SHC)			
PSY 150 General Psychology (3 SHC)			
SOC 210 Introduction to Sociology (3 SHC)			
Math (8 SHC)			
Select two courses from the following:			
MAT 171 Precalculus Algebra (4 SHC)			
MAT 172 Pre-calculus Trigonometry (4 SHC)			
MAT 263 Brief Calculus (4 SHC)			
MAT 271 Calculus I (4 SHC)			

	Credits Taken	Credits Needed	Semester/ Year
Natural Sciences (8 SHC) *Select eight SHC from the following course(s):*			

	Credits Taken	Credits Needed	Semester/ Year

Natural Sciences (8 SHC)
Select eight SHC from the following course(s):
  AST 151   General Astronomy I (3 SHC)
   and AST 151A General Astronomy Lab I (1SHC)
  BIO 110 Principles of Biology (4 SHC)
  BIO 111 General Biology I (4 SHC)
   and BIO 112 General Biology II (4 SHC)
  CHM 151 General Chemistry I (4 SHC)
   and CHM 152 General Chemistry II (4 SHC)
  GEL 111 Introductory Geology (4 SHC)
  PHY 110 Conceptual Physics (3 SHC)
   and PHY 110A Conceptual Physics Lab (1 SHC)
  PHY 151 College Physics I (4 SHC)
   and PHY 152 College Physics II (4 SHC)
  PHY 251 General Physics I (4 SHC)
   and PHY 252 General Physics II (4 SHC)			

Additional General Education Hours (11 SHC) An additional 11 SHC of courses should be selected from courses classified as general education within the Comprehensive Articulation Agreement. Students should select these courses based on their intended major and transfer university. **Total General Education Hours Required: 45**			

Other Required Hours (15 SHC)
  Academic Transition (1 SHC)
   The following course is required:
    ACA 122 College Transfer Success (1 SHC)
 	
An additional 14 SHC of courses should be selected from courses classified as pre-major, elective or general education courses within the CAA. Students should select those courses based on their intended major and transfer university.			

* One semester hour of credit may be included in a 61 SHC associate in arts program of study. The transfer of this hour is not guaranteed.			
Total Semester Hours Credit (SHC) in Program: 60-61*			

Students must meet the receiving university's foreign language and/or health and physical education requirements, if applicable, prior to or after transfer to the senior institution.

Associate in Science Academic Plan

Semester 1 _____

Course Requirement	Credits	Grade
Total Credit Hours This Semester:		

Semester 2 _____

Course Requirement	Credits	Grade
Total Credit Hours This Semester:		

Semester 3 _____

Course Requirement	Credits	Grade
Total Credit Hours This Semester:		

Semester 4 _____

Course Requirement	Credits	Grade
Total Credit Hours This Semester:		

What is your projected date of completion? _____

Chapter 4 Reflection: Course Planning and the Comprehensive Articulation Agreement (CAA)

Before you move on to the next chapter, take a moment to reflect on what you discovered in this chapter and how you can apply it to your goals.

1. What are the two most important things you learned in this chapter and how will you apply those things to your goal of transferring successfully to a four-year college or university?

2. Did your investigation of the academic training required for a degree in your field of interest provide you a clearer understanding of what you will have to commit to in order to obtain a degree? Are you willing to commit?

3. How confident are you feeling about your decision?

4. What do you need to do next?

Chapter 5
Paying for College

"In all realms of life it takes courage to stretch your limits, express your power, and fulfill your potential; it's no different in the financial realm."
— Suze Orman

In this chapter you will:

✔ Explore the Cost of College
✔ Investigate Different Sources Available to Pay for College
✔ Research Ways to Save on College Cost
✔ Create a Plan to Pay for College

Paying for College

Once you have decided on a career and the major that will best prepare you for that career, you will then begin to look at which four-year college or university has the program that fits your needs. In addition to the many other factors you must take into account when choosing the right college, you must also consider the cost. For many, cost is the deciding factor.

In this chapter you will research the total cost of your college expenses, investigate your options for paying, learn about ways to save on costs, and create an overall financial plan to pay for college. According to the College Board, the national average cost for attending college during the 2011-2012 academic year, was:

Type of College	Average Published Annual Tuition & Fees
Two-year Public (in-state)	$3,131
Four-year Public (in-state)	$8,655
Four-year Public (out-of-state)	$21,706
Four-year Private	$29,056

Associated Expenses

When you take into account how much you will have to pay to attend college, you have to consider more than the cost of tuition alone. There are many other expenses that contribute to the total cost of your education. The fees associated with these costs include, but may not be limited to:

- **Tuition & Fees:** Based on number of credit hours the student is taking per semester. May also include other miscellaneous expenses such as lab fees or student activity fees.

- **Room and Board:** Varies depending on the student living on or off the college campus.

- **Books and Supplies:** Varies depending on how many classes are taken and the required materials for each. The average yearly cost for books and supplies for a student at a four-year public college is currently between $800 and $1,100.

- **Personal Expenses:** Usually includes cost-of-living, recreation, and personal supplies. The 2011-12 national average cost for a four-year public college student living on campus is $2,066. (College Board 2011-2012)

- **Transportation:** Varies depending on how far a student must travel to and from campus, the cost of gas, bus, plane or train fare.

Colleges provide a published price, sometimes called the "Sticker Price", which includes the cost of tuition and fees, and room and board *before* factoring in grants, scholarships and financial aid awards. This amount is usually more than the student will actually have to pay. For example, you may be interested in attending a university with a published price of $7,000. After your financial aid award, the net price may be only $3,150. The "Net Price" is the total cost of tuition and fees, room and board, and books and supplies *after* the student has been awarded federal, state and college aid.

Ways to Pay

Regardless of the amount you will be expected to pay for your college education, it's imperative that you begin thinking about ways to absorb these costs. Can your family contribute? Have you been saving for college? Do you qualify for federal student aid? Financial Aid plays a pivotal role in providing access to college as well as degree completion. It is intended to make up the cost difference between what college costs and what your family can afford to pay. It is based on the premise that all students should have equal access to a college education.

Approximately two-thirds of undergraduate students receive some type of financial aid. In 2012, the average amount of financial aid that a full-time undergraduate student received was $13,200.

According to the Department of Education and FAFSA guidelines, students must meet the following eligibility requirements in order to receive federal assistance:

- Be enrolled or accepted for enrollment in an eligible program
- Have a high school diploma or GED
- Be a U.S. citizen or eligible non-citizen
- Not be a member of a religious community that directs the program of study or provides maintenance
- Be registered with the Selective Service (males only)
- Not be in default on a Title IV student loan borrowed for attendance at any institution;
- Not have borrowed in excess of Title IV loan limits
- Not owe a repayment on a Title IV grant or loan received for attendance at any institution
- Maintain satisfactory academic progress
- Not be enrolled concurrently in an elementary or secondary school
- Provide a valid social security number

If you have been convicted of possessing or selling illegal drugs, you must complete a **Drug Conviction Worksheet** to determine eligibility.

Types of Financial Aid

Grants are financial aid, based on need that you do not have to repay. Grants may be given from the federal government, state government, colleges and universities, or public or private institutions.

- **The Pell Grant** is the most well-known federal aid grant in the U.S. It began in 1972 and is one of the key areas of funding for low-income students. Eligibility for the Pell Grant is determined by family contribution, full- or part-time status, cost of attendance and length of study. This federal grant ranges from $602 to $5,550 for full-time undergraduate students and is available for a total of 12, full semesters of college attendance.

- **The Federal Supplemental Educational Opportunity Grant (FSEOG)** is another federal grant. This grant is intended to assist students who demonstrate exceptional financial need, with awards ranging from $100 to $400 per academic year. A student must have a Pell Grant to receive an FSEOG award.

There are also grants offered for different categories of students such as race, gender, area of study and military background. The key is to research all the options and apply early. Many grants have a limited amount of resources and are awarded on a first come, first served basis.

States also offer grants. It is important to research your state to see what grants may be offered. For example, North Carolina offers The NC Student Incentive Grant. To be eligible, you must:

- **be a legal resident of the state of North Carolina.**

- **be registered as a full-time student at a college within the state of North Carolina.**

- **have proof that financial help is needed.**

Scholarships are a type of grant used to finance the cost of college. They are usually awarded to undergraduate students and offer awards that don't need to be paid back.

- **Merit-based Scholarships** are awarded for outstanding academic and/or civic achievements.

- **Need-based Scholarships** are awarded on the basis of the financial need of the student. These type of scholarships require applicants to fill out the Free Application for Federal Student Aid (FAFSA).

- **Combination of Merit and Need or Competitive** can be based on academic excellence, civic achievement, leadership qualities and athletic ability.

General scholarships have a broad nature and can be offered by any individual or organization for various amounts. Scholarships can also be program or major specific. Just remember that there are businesses and organizations in your communities that are interested in recognizing local students by sponsoring scholarships for college. It would be in your best interest to check into local scholarships. An effective search can render scholarships that are specific to a student's skills and interests.

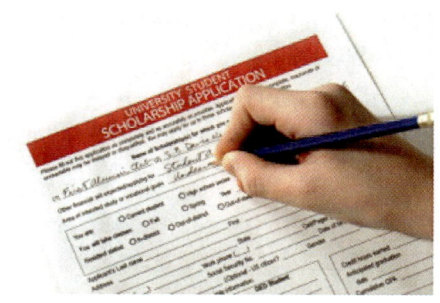

Ways to Find Scholarships

- **Colleges and Universities** disburse the majority of scholarships available to students. A great place to search is at the four-year colleges that interest you. Also check with the department of your major. There may be scholarships or grants available to students specific to some career fields.

- **Libraries typically** reserve numerous books about financial aid and scholarship guides.

- **Advisors and Counselors** usually maintain a current collection of books and brochures on scholarships and grants. They can also be helpful with effective application strategies.

- **Online** there are many websites available to help you find scholarships, grants, and loans that match your skills, interests, talents, and financial background. Be cautious of scholarship sites that offer information for a fee.

- **Community Organizations and Foundations** often offer scholarships to students for outstanding scholastic achievements, leadership and civic engagement.

- **Companies/Employers** sometimes offer scholarships, partial- or full-tuition reimbursement to their employees and the children of their employees.

- **The Federal Student Aid Information Center** may be called at 1.800.4.FED.AID.

- **The College/University Financial Aid Office** usually has a list of all scholarships offered to the students attending that institution.

Collegeboard.org reports that almost three billion dollars in scholarships is available for college students every year. Many four-year colleges and universities offer scholarships that specifically target transfer students. Make sure that you ask about the possibilities when you are researching your prospective four-year colleges.

Federal College Loans are what students and their families depend more on than any other source of financial aid. More than $100 billion in federal education loans and $10 billion in private student loans are originated each year.

Educational loans are like other loans—you have to repay the money you borrow with interest. However there are some differences in these loans compared to traditional loans.
For example, you do not have to make payments while you are in college and usually start repaying 6-9 months after you graduate or stop taking classes. Also these loans traditionally have lower interest rates and you don't need a credit history to qualify.

There are Three General Types of Loans Offered:

- **Federal Direct Subsidized Stafford Loans**
  These loans are based on financial need. Subsidized means that the government will pay the interest on the loan while the student is in school

- **Federal Direct Unsubsidized Stafford Loans**
  Students get Federal Direct Unsubsidized Stafford Loans regardless of need, but will have to pay all interest charges.

- **Federal Direct PLUS Loans (Parent Loans for Undergraduate Students)**
  Parents of dependent students can borrow a Federal Direct PLUS Loan to help pay for their child's education.

Your college education is an investment that will pay off in the long run in terms of a better paying career. In the short term, loans are often a necessary option to help pay for college. The majority of college students will require student loans to help meet their educational expenses, and the average four-year college graduate has more than $25,000 in student loan debt. Knowing all of this, it is important to keep in mind that the amount of debt you have upon graduation can have a significant impact on your lifestyle after college. The question of how much to borrow needs to be carefully considered. According to Central Piedmont Community College financial aid department, following are some tips for managing your student loan debt.

- **Do Not Over Borrow!** Borrow only what you need for your current school year educational expenses. If your expenses increase later, you can always request a second loan application up to your maximum eligibility.

- **Calculate Final Student Loan Debt Total.** Consider how much you will need to borrow to meet all of your educational goals, whether it's for an associate, bachelor's or masters degree, or beyond.

- **Consider monthly payment totals.** Calculate what your monthly payments will be on the loan when it comes time to repay the loan. Do you feel this monthly amount will be doable?

- **Estimate what other expenses you will have after graduation.** What will be the costs of your housing, food, transportation, insurance, credit cards, car payments, etc.

- **Consider what the average starting salary is for the career field you plan to enter.** Based on this salary do you feel comfortable with this loan debt? Also consider what the job outlook is for your career field. Where would be the best place to live upon graduation? Are you willing to move if necessary?

- **Resist the temptation to use your student loans for other things beyond your immediate educational expenses.**

The Federal Work Study Program and Student Employment

A great way to help subsidize the cost of college is to obtain employment. There are work programs available that are conducive to a college student's needs. Most any student, regardless of their financial status, can find on-campus work that coincides with their career goals. Some university programs and departments hire students as lab assistants, researchers and more. Experience working in these areas will increase your knowledge base, expand your network and help you polish your soft skills. The wages for these jobs are often competitive with the national minimum wage.

- **The Federal Work Study Program** is a federally funded employment program which provides on-campus part-time employment for students, allowing them to earn a portion of education expenses while attending college. Students must qualify for financial aid in order to be eligible for this program. The colleges/universities are responsible for administering the Federal Work Study Program. Awards vary based on student need and the institution's funding level.

- **Student Work Programs** are part-time employment positions available to college students on the university campus. They too offer a competitive wage and are conducive to a college student's needs. Students are not required to be receiving financial aid in order to secure these positions.

- **Leadership Stipends** are sometimes provided to students that hold leadership positions at their respective university/college. Some leadership positions include, but are not limited to, those in the Student Government Association, Residence Life/Housing, New Student Orientation and Greek Life.

All of these work options on college campuses can contribute to a rich college experience while helping you gain valuable skills that will transfer into your preferred career after college. There is also employment available outside of your college campuses but these jobs may not be as flexible with you during academic intense periods like mid-term, final exams or when you need to work on a term paper.

What Role Does Your Family Play in Paying for College

The expected family contribution (EFC) is the amount that your family is able to pay toward the cost of your college education. It is usually determined by the federal government or the prospective college. A formula uses the information you report on the FAFSA to analyze and compare your family's financial conditions with other families' financial conditions.

This formula calculates the EFC that your family can contribute by evaluating your income, assets and family size. The expectation is that a combination of savings, current income and possibly borrowing will help your family meet the EFC. The Financial Aid Office determines your eligibility for financial aid by taking the EFC number to determine a student's financial need. The formula used by the financial office is to subtract the expected family contribution from the cost to attend college (COA) to determine the student's financial need.

Considering the family's role in paying for your college education also means having a conversation with your parent(s) or guardian(s) about the cost, what is affordable and who will pay. You need to know the family's financial status and if there have been provisions made to help pay for your education.

A great way to get the dialogue started is to inform your parents that you have decided to go to college and you would like to discuss some of your options with them. Ask for their opinion on your decision to go. This may encourage them to bring up the issue of money themselves.

Here are some talking points for the conversation about money:

- Can we afford to pay for college?

- Is there a college fund or savings committed to my education?

- Can you afford to pay the expected family contribution and how much can you afford to commit yearly?

- Are you willing to apply for a PLUS loan to help me pay for college?

- Does your employer offer scholarships for the children of their employees?

- Can I afford to attend a private college or should I pursue a public education?

- Can I afford to attend a college out of state?

- Are you aware of any scholarships from any civic or community organizations that I might qualify for?

What if Your Family Can't Help Pay for College

Parents having the primary responsibility of paying for their child's education is what federal student aid programs base a student's dependent or independent classification on. If the student is found to be a dependent they <u>must</u> report their parent(s) income as well as their own information on the FAFSA.

Independent status is not granted to a student living outside of the parent's home for financial aid purposes. However, there are exceptions which include:

- The event in which a student is severely estranged from their parent(s) due to an extenuating circumstance such as physical or emotional abuse, severe estrangement or abandonment, etc.

In these cases the student will be able to pursue a "Dependency Override" (an appeal of the dependency status) and will need to provide three letters or documents confirming that validity of their claim.

According to the Department of Education and FAFSA guidelines, in order to be declared an independent, the student must provide specified documentation supporting the request for change of status.

You should also be aware that there are conditions that do not warrant independent or self-supporting status. These conditions include if the parent(s):

- refuses to contribute to the student's education.
- refuses to provide required information.
- lives out-of-state.
- has/have iexhausted his/her income.

Or if the student:

- elects not to live with the parents and/or with other relatives.
- elects not to have communication with the parents.
- demonstrates total self-sufficiency.

One of the strongest financial investments that you will make in your lifetime is the cost of your college education. In order to generate the best return on your investment, careful planning is a must. Remember, you must take a good, hard look at the money issues concerning the cost of college.

Ways to Reduce Costs

- Attend a Community College for your general education requirements.
- Take the maximum number of courses you can handle each semester and graduate on time.
- Consider attending a local university and commute from home.
- Buy used books or shop for reduced prices online.
- Create a budget for your personal expenses and set spending limits for yourself.
- Look for campus employment and leadership opportunities that pay stipends and offer remissions.

Quick Tips

1. **Everyone should fill out the FAFSA.**
   You should submit the FAFSA as soon as possible after January 1. Even if you think you will not qualify for financial aid due to your income, do it anyway. Many scholarships require the FAFSA to be completed as part of the application process as well.

2. **Meeting deadlines is paramount.**
   Make sure you meet any deadlines for financial aid, including scholarships and grants. Check with your college to make sure you have exact dates, including any priority deadlines. Those students who meet these deadlines are considered first for financial aid.

3. **Know what resources are available to you.**
   If you are not sure at any time, meet with a financial aid advisor at your college. Ask lots of questions. Use www.collegeboard.org and other websites to gather information.

4. **Find out exactly how much the college costs that you want to attend.**
   Go to the Collegeboard.com site and use their College Cost Calculator. You can total up all your costs and subtract your expected financial aid. This will give you a great target of the actual out of pocket costs you can expect.

5. **Remember the 12 semester limit for financial aid.**
   Plan your courses and your finances to ensure you have enough financial aid to cover all the semesters you will need to complete your degree.

Exercise 5.1: Financial Plan for College

This worksheet will assist you in your financial planning for college. Visit www.collegeboard.org and the website for one of your top college choices to help you complete this worksheet. If you cannot find the answers to the questions on the college website, contact the college directly for an interview with a member of the financial aid staff.

I. Name of College _____

1. What's the average cost a student at this institution pays annually for tuition and fees, books and supplies, room and board, travel, and other personal expenses combined?

2. Has there been a tuition increase in the past three years? Is there an increase expected within the next four years?

3. What are the different types of financial aid offered at this university?

4. What is the priority deadline to apply for financial aid and when are students notified about financial aid award decisions?

5. If a student is not granted enough financial aid to cover the cost to attend this university, what other options are there?

6. How does the financial aid package change from year-to-year (less/more)? What are the academic requirements or other conditions for the renewal of financial aid, including scholarships?

7. What happens if your financial aid package is not ready before it's time to register and pay for classes?

8. If you are not granted financial aid of any kind, how will you be billed by the college? Will you have to pay the total sum or is there an option to spread the yearly payment out over equal monthly installments?

II. One of the ways to reduce college cost is to begin your journey at a community college where the cost is typically lower than four-year colleges/universities. Let's start by looking at the cost you've incurred this semester and the sources from which you paid them.

Cost Description	Amount	Your Contribution
Tuition and Fees		
Room/Rent		
Board/Food	$250/MONTH	
Books and Supplies		
Transportation	$100/MONTH	
Personal Expenses	~SEE $15/mo, $10/mo TOILETRIES $50/mo CLOTHING	
Other Costs		
Totals		

III. What is the breakdown of the yearly cost for your first choice transfer university?

Cost Description	Amount
Tuition and Fees	
Room/Board	
Books and Supplies	
Transportation	
Personal Expenses	
Other Costs	
Totals	

4, 5 mo NTH SEMESTERS

IV. What is the total cost for your bachelor's degree? Total up the number of years it will take and multiply that by the cost per year.

$

V. Now that you have a general idea of how much college will cost and the different resources available to help pay for college, what resources do you anticipate using to pay for college?

1.

2.

3.

4.

5.

Chapter 5 Reflection: Paying for College

Before you move ahead to the next chapter, take a moment to reflect on what you discovered in this chapter and how you can apply it to your goal of transferring.

1. What are the three most important things you learned in this chapter and how will you apply those things to your goal of transferring successfully to a four-year college or university?

2. Were there any surprises about the cost of college and your options to pay? What are they and how did they compare to your expectations?

3. What is the next step that you need to take to secure financing for college and how will you implement it?

Chapter 6
The Admissions Process

"You have brains in your head.
You have feet in your shoes.
You can steer yourself in any direction you choose.
You're on your own.
And you know what you know.
You are the guy who'll decide where to go."
— Dr. Seuss

In this chapter you will:

✔ Research the College Admissions Process and Requirements

✔ Review the 10 Ways to Tackle the Admissions Process

✔ Conduct an Information Interview

✔ Create Your Admissions Campaign and Timeline

The Admissions Process

So far in this course you have selected your career and major, completed your program evaluation, and researched your financial options for the next step in your educational journey.

In this chapter, you will create a Personal Admissions Campaign and Timeline to use as you apply to your selected colleges. You will conduct an information interview, understand the admissions requirements for your top three schools and then create a tracking system to ensure you are meeting all deadlines for admissions and financial aid.

After interviewing admissions counselors and other professionals from more than 20 different colleges and universities, we have created a list of the Top 10 Tips to consider as you begin the admissions process. Before you start your official campaign, take a look and see how these tips can make your admissions journey more successful.

10 Ways to Tackle College Admissions

1. **Visit the top two or three campuses you are interested in attending.** One of the biggest mistakes students make is not visiting a college before attending. Don't plan to make your final college selection without visiting at least your top two or three choices. You would not buy a house without looking at it, would you? How serious are you about choosing the best college for yourself?

   Sign up for a tour of the campus and ask if you can attend a class. Always take along another pair of eyes and ears and ask as many questions as possible about the college, the atmosphere and the classes. There is nothing like the gut feeling you have when you walk around the campus and talk with individuals at the school.

2. **Conduct an information interview with a member of the faculty or admissions to learn more about academic life at this college.** Some questions to consider include: What is the average class size? Are faculty teaching courses in my major or are they being taught by graduate students? Are faculty members accessible and supportive? What types of counseling, tutoring and career services support are provided here? Does the college offer any special orientation or transition support for transfer students?

3. **Talk to graduates of the colleges you are considering.** Why did they choose this college? Did it prepare them adequately for their career? What would they do differently today? Would they recommend this college's program to an individual pursuing your career path?

4. **Evaluate how successful you will be at this college.** Ask yourself: Why are you going to college? Keep asking yourself this question. How will this specific school help you build your future and maximize opportunities in your career? Are you prepared for the academic rigor and requirements to graduate? Does the college offer opportunities for extracurricular activities that support your growth as a student and community member? Can you see yourself spending time here comfortably and graduating from this university?

5. **Consider your finances.** Create a plan of how you will pay for your education. Have you applied for all financial aid and scholarships that are available? Does the college have any special scholarships for transfer students? Do you plan to live on campus? Will you be working while in college? Are there any on campus work study programs available? Planning realistically now will make you more comfortable when the final decisions have to be made.

6. **Remember that application deadlines are not suggestions.** Whether it's for admissions, SAT or ACT registration, financial aid, scholarships, or campus housing, never miss the deadlines. Missing deadlines will likely have negative results. Create a calendar and adhere strictly to all deadlines. Get organized by creating a file for each college you are applying to. Be prepared for the workload of completing your applications and gathering all the documents you will need.

7. **Start saving early for application fees.** This is often an overlooked step. You do not want to miss a deadline due to lack of funds for the application. The average application fee for colleges in the United States is approximately $40. Keep in mind there are many schools that will waive the fee for students with financial need, while others offer a waiver to students who apply online.

8. **Make sure you know exactly what is required for the admission packet.** What type of application must be submitted? Will you be required to apply to the college of your major in addition to general admission to the university? Do you need transcripts from your community college or high school? Is an essay required? Do you need references or letters of recommendation? Plan early.

9. **Talk to your community college professors or academic advisors about which colleges may be a good fit for you.** Choose one or two faculty who may be able to write a letter or recommendation for you if needed. The faculty should know you well enough to speak about your academic record, specific examples of how you performed in class and about your motivation and character. Be sure to follow up with deadline reminders to anyone you ask for a recommendation.

10. **When making your final choice, seek the advice of family and counselors about where you should apply.** Discuss your college options with those who know you well and whose judgment you value. They can help you sort through the options and give you different perspectives.

When it comes down to the final decision on where to apply, more than anything else, you should be yourself throughout the admissions and selection process. Think about your passion and what drives you. Show who you are and how you will contribute to the learning community at the university. Colleges want to have a variety of students from different backgrounds and varied experiences.

So let's say that you've decided to apply to transfer to five colleges/universities. Three of the five are your top choices and two are back-up colleges just in case your top choices don't work out. Just remember that the application process can be taxing as well as exhausting. In some cases the admissions processes are designed this way to weed out those without the intellectual savvy and organizational skills to navigate their way through the process. Be sure that you develop a well-organized search and application process.

> ### To Organize Your Search
> - **Create an electronic folder for each college to which you plan to apply**
> - **Create a sub folder for each of the following: application, references, financial aid, transcripts, essays, housing and contacts**
> - **Make sure that you include a check list of tasks with the correct dates and deadlines**
> - **Update files every time you complete a task**
> - **Always have a back-up copy of everything**

A well-organized admissions campaign will save you time and frustration, as well as help you make the right decision on where to transfer.

Electronic Applications
Today most college admission application processes are electronic.

- Make sure you have proofed and have run spellcheck on all of your information before you submit your application.
- Use a secure computer to protect sensitive and confidential information.
- Don't leave any blanks on the application; enter N/A for non-applicable when a question does not apply.
- Protect and keep track of all passwords.
- Try to finish the application in one sitting and use high-speed Internet connection.
- Always print a hard copy of the application for your personal files.
- Read through the entire application before you click submit.
- Print a copy of the confirmation that your application has been received.
- Once filed, check your email daily for college communications; follow directions and deadlines to the letter.
- Make sure that you have respectable email addresses and voicemail messages on your phones.

Transcripts

You will be required to submit official copies of your transcripts to each college you apply to for admission. This means that you'll need to make a formal request to all of your former schools, any community or four-year colleges at which you have taken classes and maybe even your high school transcripts.

- Find out how the college defines the term "Official Transcripts" - usually means sealed with the college's official seal.

- Find out whether transcripts must be sent directly from the college to the admissions office or attached to a transcript form.

- Check the number of transcripts required from each school.

- Always check to make sure that the admissions office has received your official copy.

Letters of Recommendation

- Use former community college professors that can attest to your level of commitment and academic performance. Advisors for your civic/leadership engagements are strong references as well.

- Get permission from your references to use them and provide all of your pertinent information and deadlines.

- Make sure you give the references enough time to complete and submit your request.

- Contact references with a reminder a week before the deadline and ask if additional information is needed.

- Always send a thank you to your references.

Essays

Many times when you have completed the minimum course requirement for transfer to a four-year college/university, there is no essay requirement for admission. However, you may come across a college that does require one. Admissions essays are an important piece of the admissions process. It is an opportunity for you to show off your skills, strengths and talents.

Most colleges want to know how attending their college will benefit you and play an active role in your career and life goals. You may also have a chance to tell your unique story and motivation to pursue your career interests. This is a good opportunity for you to explain any special circumstances/issues in your academic past. For example – why you had low grades at an earlier time in college or why you dropped classes during the middle of the semester.

Make sure when you are writing your admissions essay you maintain your integrity. Be authentic and true to who you are.

Remember your application is not complete until the admissions department has everything submitted. Contact the college directly to ensure your application is complete.

Admissions Essay Writing Tips

- *Attend a writing workshop.*

- *Brainstorm ideas and create an outline before you begin the essay.*

- *Open with a strong statement.*

- *Give examples that support your positions and prove your points.*

- *Conclude your essay by summarizing your opening and body, then state your conclusion.*

- *Have a community college advisor proof your work and give you feedback.*

- *Read it out loud to yourself.*

- *State how your major at this college will help you reach career and life goals.*

- *If necessary, show evidence of grade improvements.*

How to Conduct an Admissions Information Interview

As part of your overall admissions campaign, you will be researching your top three colleges. You may start with online research at the school's website for some of the questions and then confirm or go into more detail as needed by speaking personally to someone from the college. You may choose to interview an admissions counselor or ask these questions when you make one of your campus visits. How you gather the information is up to you.

Listed below are some suggestions for questions to ask. Feel free to add additional questions based on your personal needs and interests.

General Information and Campus Life

1. What is the mission of the college?

2. Does the college/university accept transfer students?

3. Does the college/university have my major? Is my major accredited?

4. How many credits are required to transfer? (minimum and maximum)?

5. What is my estimated graduation date from this college/university?

6. What are the benefits to attending this college/university?

7. What is campus life like?

8. What is the demographic break down of the student population?

9. Is this a residential campus? Can transfer students live on campus?

10. What is the average class size for my major? Are classes in my major taught by faculty or graduate assistants?

11. What are some ways in which this college maintains strong connections with the workforce and community?

12. What sources of financial aid are available to transfer students? Do you have any special scholarships for transfer students?

13. What other advice would you give me in terms of admissions and transferring successfully to your school?

Admissions Requirements

1. How much is the application fee?

2. What type of application must be submitted (the college's app., system-wide, the common Transfer app., or department app.)?

3. What transcripts are required?

4. Are references or recommendation letters required (How many?)

5. Is an essay required? (What is the essay topic?)

6. Is a portfolio required? What elements are needed or recommended?

7. Is an interview required or recommended? Is this in person or via phone? Is this with an individual or panel?

8. Is the application deadline fixed or rolling?

9. What's the minimum GPA requirement? What's the competitive GPA?

10. Are there additional requirements to be accepted into my major?

11. Do I need an SAT/ACT score for admission? What is the competitive score?

12. What else would you like to add?

Quick Tips

1. **Schedule a campus visit.**
   Remember being in the physical campus environment can be the best way to get a feel for the school and decide if it is right for you.

2. **Ask questions.**
   You can talk to alumni, your professors and friends, students currently at the college and admissions officers. Talk to as many people as you can about the college options you are considering. This will help you make the most informed decision.

3. **Get clear on the admission requirements.**
   Create a file for each school and make sure you are observing all deadlines. Also give yourself plenty of time to submit a strong application. Don't force a rushed application because you waited until the deadlines were upon you to begin working on them.

4. **Make sure you have a backup plan.**
   Apply to more than one school so you can ensure you have alternative options if needed... just in case your first choice doesn't work out.

Exercise 6.1: Transfer Admissions Campaign

Your College Transfer Admissions Campaign is a systematic process course of aggressive activities and actions for the purpose of gaining admission into the senior college/university you desire. It can also be considered your marketing plan. For the purpose of this class, you will be designing your own individual Transfer Admissions Campaign.

The steps include: naming and creating the goal for your campaign, managing and tracking your campaign; and summarizing your campaign.

Naming and Creating a Goal for Your Campaign: Here you will come up with a creative name for your campaign and establish your goal. Remember, when establishing your campaign goal, you need to use the SMART method of goal setting. Make sure your goal is specific, measurable, attainable, realistic and timely.

Campaign Name and Goal

Campaign Name	Type the name of the new campaign.
Campaign Goal	Type the name of the campaign goal.
Start Date	
End Date	
Two College Choices	
Notes	

Managing and Tracking Your Campaign: This involves researching the admission requirements and associated deadlines for the selected colleges. In this phase, you will have to create a timeline of events to be completed for your campaign and manage those things that need to be done.

Summarizing Your Campaign: After you have researched all of the requirements for admission to your intended colleges, you will begin summarizing your campaign. In this phase, you summarize your findings and make decisions based on what you have found. Once you have completed this exercise, complete the Chapter 5 Reflection based on your findings.

First Choice

Name of College:	Location:
Major/Minor:	Cost Per Year:

Admissions Requirements

Item	Required Y/N	Method	Deadline	Completed Y/N
Application(Cost)		Electronic, paper		
Test scores (number of copies)				
Official Transcripts (number of copies)				
References/ Recommendation Letters				
Admission Essay		Topic:		
Personal Interview				
Campus Housing Application				
Financial Aid Application				
Scholarship Applications				
GPA Requirement	List minimum and competitive			
Credits Required	What is the minimum number of credits required			
Notes/Special Instructions				

Second Choice

Name of College:	Location:
Major/Minor:	Cost Per Year:

Admissions Requirements

Item	Required Y/N	Method	Deadline	Completed Y/N
Application(Cost)		Electronic, paper		
Test scores (number of copies)				
Official Transcripts (number of copies)				
References/ Recommendation Letters				
Admission Essay		Topic:		
Personal Interview				
Campus Housing Application				
Financial Aid Application				
Scholarship Applications				
GPA Requirement	List minimum and competitive			
Credits Required	What is the minimum number of credits required			
Notes/Special Instructions				

Chapter 6 Reflection: Admissions Process

Before you move on to the next chapter, take a moment to reflect on what you discovered in this chapter and how you can apply it to your goals.

1. What are the two most important things you learned in this chapter and how will you apply those things to your goal of transferring successfully to a four-year college or university?

2. Do you feel you have created an admission campaign that reflects your best college options with an achievable timeline and plan? Why or why not?

3. What concerns do you have at this point about your admissions campaign?

4. Create a "To-do" list of the next five things you need to do based on your campaign findings.

Chapter 7
Making the Transition

"Begin with the end in mind." — Stephen Covey

In this chapter you will:

✔ Make Your Final College Choice
✔ Identify a Plan B
✔ Create Your Personal Mission Statement
✔ Prepare a Transition Plan

Making the Transition

Congratulations! You have researched and planned and are now ready to make your final decision on where you will continue your education. Let's take a moment to revisit the objectives for this class and the five Steps to Transfer Success.

Step 1
You have assessed yourself and chosen your major.

Step 2
You have explored college culture, identified your individual college needs, identified the best colleges for your career choice and major, and learned about course planning.

Step 3
You then researched the cost of attending college, identified different sources available to help pay for college and learned about some ways that you can save on the cost of college.

Step 4
You explored the college admissions requirements and conducted informational interviews with your top college choices.

Step 5
In this chapter you will begin to evaluate your transfer college options, make a decision on which will be your best fit and prepare for a successful transition to your transfer college/university.

> **Five Steps to Transfer Success**
>
> 1. **Choosing the Right Major for Your Career**
>
> 2. **Understanding College Culture and Your Personal Needs**
>
> 3. **Researching Finance Options to Pay for Your Four-Year College**
>
> 4. **Creating a Personal Admissions Campaign**
>
> 5. **Making Your Choice and Making the Transition**

Begin With the End in Mind

Before you make your final decision, let's step back a minute and reflect on who you are and what legacy you want to leave behind. Let's start by writing your personal mission statement.

Imagine you are 90 years old, sitting on a rocking chair on your porch. You are happy and pleased with your life. Looking back on all that you've achieved and acquired, all the relationships you've developed, what matters to you most? How would you like to be remembered for?

In his book "The Seven Habits of Highly Effective People," Stephen Covey lists habit two as "Begin With the End in Mind." Often we go through life reacting to the things that happen to us and allowing other people to make decisions for us about what is important and what we should do with our lives. We may achieve great things but these can also come at the expense of things that are more valuable to us. Covey says, "If the ladder is not leaning against the right wall, every step we take just gets us to the wrong place faster."

According to Covey, "Begin with the end in mind" is based on the principle that all things are created twice. There is a mental (first) creation, and a physical (second) creation." (Covey, 1989) The physical creation comes after the mental creation similar to how a building follows a blueprint. You must make a conscious effort to visualize who you are and what you want in life; otherwise, you are allowing other people and circumstances to shape you and your life by default. You need to connect to what makes you unique and then define the personal, moral and ethical guidelines within which you can most happily express and fulfill yourself. You can use these guidelines to set your goals, make important decisions in your life and decide how you will use your time, energy and talents.

One of the best ways to ensure your life has clear direction and purpose is to develop a Personal Mission Statement. It will focus on what you want to be and do. It is your plan for success. It reaffirms who you are and puts your goals in focus. Your mission statement makes you the leader of your own life. It is the criterion by which you measure everything else in your life.

Historically, mission statements have defined the purposes of many of the world's greatest institutions and companies. For example, Coca Cola's mission is: "Refresh the world, inspire moments of optimism and happiness, and create value and make a difference." Why not use this same premise to help you define your purpose in life? On the next page are some strong reasons why you should invest in creating your own personal mission statement.

Creating You Own Personal Mission Statement Can Help:

- **Identify what you value:** What is important to you and what is your moral compass?

- **Identify what you believe in:** What are your principles and what do you stand for?

- **Identify your purpose in life:** What is your essential mission in life? What are you passionate about and who do you want to be?

- **Identify your personal responsibility to yourself and others:** How do you get to where you want to go and who's accountable for making it happen? What causes do you believe in? Who do you want to help?

- **Establish your personal and professional goals.** Are my daily decisions aligned with my mission? Are my goals helping me reach my mission?

A great example of a public mission statement was made back in 1960, when John F. Kennedy said that we would put a man on the moon by the end of the decade. He had a clear goal with a specific timeline for its achievement. Despite many obstacles, in 1969, Neil Armstrong had taken that one big step and helped Kennedy achieve his mission.

Writing Your Mission Statement

In her book "The Path," Laurie Beth Jones says, "The truth is that all great leaders in history have had missions that were no longer than one sentence long. Abraham Lincoln's mission was to preserve the Union. FDR's was to end the Depression. Nelson Mandela's mission was to end apartheid. Mother Teresa's mission was to show mercy and compassion to the dying. A good mission statement is so easily communicated and understood that a 12 year old can understand and repeat it." (Jones, 1996)

There are many ways and formats you can use to write your mission statement. Some people write a four-five sentence version, some write a paragraph, and some write a one sentence declaration that they can easily memorize. Do what works for you.

- Write a statement or paragraph that will define your purpose and mission in life.
- Consider stating the career you desire and what makes you passionate about that career.
- Think about the mark you want to make on the world and how you want to be perceived by the rest of the world.
- Consider the roles you play in your life.
- Personalize it—make it meaningful and easy to remember.
- Answer the important questions from the "Asking the Right Questions" activity.
- Be visionary and self-inspired.

Mission Statement Examples

A. It is my personal mission to become an outstanding physician of Obstetrics and Gynecology and surgeon. I wish to return to my home in Djibouti to provide effective medical treatment to women whom have suffered from female genital mutilation. I want to help restore the spirit and heal the wounds of victims of violent crimes against women. I also endeavor to fight to have the practice of FMG abolished in my country and the world. (Mission Statement of ACA 122 student at CPCC, Fall 2010)

B. Anonymous example of a mission statement:

- My mission is to give, for giving is what I do best and I can learn to do better.

- I will seek to learn, for learning is the basis for growth, and growing is the key to living. I will seek first to understand, for understanding is the key to finding value, and value is the basis for respect, decisions, and action. This should be my first act with my wife, my family and my business.

- I want to help influence the future development of people and organizations. I want to teach my children and others to love and laugh, to learn and grow beyond their current bounds.

- I will build personal, business and civic relationships by giving, in frequent little ways.

What Do We Do With It?

- **Take pride and ownership in your personal mission statement.** Put it on display or in a special place. You should look at it weekly to keep yourself motivated and on track.

- **Allow humble self-analysis of your personal growth and development.** Use this to reflect on what yet needs to be done and the achievements accomplished to this point in time.

- **Always allow room for revising.** As life's experiences provoke growth and change, expect to make adjustments to your goals and desires, as they will shift with age.

Making the Right Decision

Once you have been accepted to one or more of the colleges to which you have applied, you will be faced with the big decision of which is the best college for you. If needed, refer back to the decision making worksheet (Chapter 2) to help you to make the right decision. To also help you with this, evaluate the following factors:

- How do you feel about the college in general?
- Is this the right college culture?
- What's the size of the student body? Is the campus size ideal?
- Did you get accepted into your major?
- How large or small are the classes?
- How many of your community college credits will this college accept?
- When will you be able to graduate?
- Did you visit the campus and how was it?
- How much financial aid and scholarships will you get?
- How much out of pocket cost is involved?
- What is the housing situation? Will it fit your needs?

Get an Official Report of the Credits That Will Transfer

With the cost of college being so expensive today you need to have a clear understanding of exactly how many college credits you have remaining and how many years it will take you to graduate. Before you make your decision to attend any of the colleges that you've been accepted to, you need to request an official report of which courses you will get credit for from your community college, and how they will count toward your major, general education requirements or electives.

Don't be afraid to negotiate any courses that are not accepted at the four-year university. You might be surprised at how far a well-researched justification can get you. Always look at the course descriptions and compare to the descriptions of the classes you have taken. You may be able to convince the advisor to consider the option for a course requirement or as an elective.

What is Your Plan B?

Considering that the demand for jobs today promotes an employer's market, it would behoove any student to pursue studies at the universities with strongest programs for your major in the state and in some cases the nation. Sometimes despite your best efforts, things don't work out as you planned. In such cases, everyone should have a "Plan B." Plan B is a popular term used to mean a reserved, secondary plan, in case a first plan (a hypothetical "Plan A.") fails.

- Apply to more than your top transfer college choices. Have at least two to three fall-back options.
- Sometimes if you don't get in on your first try you can take courses at the college to demonstrate that you can handle the workload then stress your efforts when you reapply.

College Road Map

As you think about the next two to four years, the following checklist will prove helpful to you in terms of planning the key activities you may want to do each year to prepare for your life after college. This document is designed to work as a guide toward your college success. Feel free to add additional items that may pertain to your individual collegiate journey.

First Year: Acclimating Yourself to College Life

- Set goals for the year.
- Get to know yourself and how you fit into college life.
- Explore your academic and extracurricular interests.
- Adjust to your new environment and the freedom/responsibility that go along with it.
- Assess your study skills and habits – improve them if they need work.
- Figure out the difference in the academic demands from your previous school and find resources that will contribute to your success.
- Explore clubs and organizations that interest you.
- Talk to other students for advice about their majors, classes and professors.
- Start to become aware of people in roles who are doing work that is interesting to you.
- Consider a job, an internship or a volunteer experience in an area that interests you.
- Begin researching career and major possibilities.
- Enroll in a transfer degree program.
- Begin researching prospective senior colleges and request admissions information.

Second Year: Exploring Careers and Majors

- Set goals for the year.
- Meet with your faculty advisor to discuss majors and course planning options. Establish your academic plan.
- Establish a strong relationship with career services and find out what insights they provide on career direction. Map out your career plan. Conduct a more detailed exploration of occupations and possibilities. Identify possible career field options.

- Learn how to network and cultivate mentors. Start attending networking events. Create a tracking system for your contacts. Attend career fairs and workshops and start making contacts.
- Conduct informational interviews with people working in career fields that interest you.
- Get more invested in leadership opportunities and extracurricular activities. Find out what organizations related to your career/major exist. Consider running for an executive position within an organization.
- Start exploring service learning/volunteer opportunities. Get hands-on experience by using your breaks and vacations to volunteer and intern.
- Select your major and concentration or minor.
- Keep a journal of your experiences and the skills you are gaining while in college.
- Begin looking into graduate schools and requirements (exams, GPA requirements, costs, fellowships etc.).
- Decide on the transfer colleges you will apply to.
- Meet with your faculty advisor to make sure you are on schedule to graduate/transfer.
- Conduct campus visits for top college transfer choices.
- Plan living arrangements for next year.
- Apply for graduation at your community college.

Third Year: Building Your Marketing Plan

- Set goals for career related interning, externing, volunteering, and summer job experience. Everything that you do should be geared toward the career path you've chosen. Talk to prospective employers about possible jobs and internships and be willing to accept non-paying positions.
- Prioritize your interests and begin creating your career marketing plan. Build a portfolio.
- Choose academic electives that enhance your learning and career goals.
- Get a head start on preparing for grad school admissions processes. Take any grad school exams (LSAT, MCAT, GRE etc.). This will allow time to retake if needed.
- Conduct career research. Target and research potential employers/companies and areas that you wish to pursue your career with.
- Hone your job search skills and techniques (communication, interpersonal, research, networking, interviewing). Start working closely with career services to create a solid résumé and get it out there. Practice and improve your interviewing skills. Start working on your interview attire. Update résumé to reflect current experiences.
- Increase your networking skills.
- Start connecting with alumni in your field of interest.
- Reassess your extracurricular activities. Look for more challenging opportunities.
- Continually refine your job search or graduate school plans.
- Plan your senior year and create a To Do/Check List. This will help to minimize possible stress during your senior year.

Fourth Year: Transitioning to Life After College

- Meet with your advisor to make sure that you're on track to graduate this year.
- Apply for graduation.
- Network and make the most of your college's career fairs, forums, and employment readiness workshops. Consider volunteering for some of the events to gain the inside track.
- Research potential employers. Identify relevant periodicals and trade journals. Bone up on new trends in your specialty area. Develop a job search strategy.
- Visit career services. Brush up on your interviewing skills and refine your résumé.
- Get your interviewing attire together.
- Clean up your online image. Make sure you Google yourself and check your Facebook, Twitter and other online profiles.
- Apply to graduate school if you're planning to go.
- Make contact with your references, get their permission to use their names and obtain the correct contact information for them.
- Plan to make your transition to life after college. Where will you live? How will you get to work? What if the job you really want doesn't work out? What is your back-up plan?
- Take your finals and graduate!

Transitioning Successfully

You are ready to go. Let's take a minute to think about the actual transition you are about to make and honor some of the things you may be feeling about this upcoming change in your life. To do this we will use a model developed by William Bridges in 1991 called the Transitions Model. Bridges says that during times of transition we go through certain steps in our minds and he breaks these down into three stages:

1. Endings
2. Neutral Zone
3. New Beginnings

Stage 1: Endings, Losing and Letting Go

This is the initial stage of transition in which you are presented with change to what has been familiar and comfortable. You are familiar with your current college campus and know where all of the classrooms and offices are located. You have built relationships with instructors, college professionals and fellow students. The prospect of letting go of this environment might be met with some resistance.

During the Endings you may feel:

1. fear, denial or anger.
2. sadness or disorientation.
3. frustration or uncertainty.

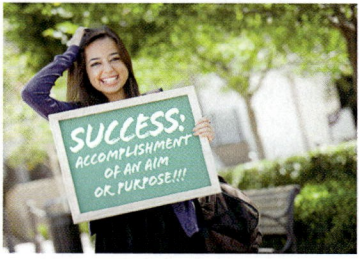

To help ease the transition:

- communicate what you are feeling.

- be proud of your accomplishment and embrace the change.

- establish support with other students who are experiencing this stage.

- identify and utilize the resources available to help you succeed in the new environment, such as visiting the transfer resources center at your college and attending a students in transition orientation.

- polish up your knowledge and skills by taking advantage of training or learning opportunities.

Stage 2: Neutral Zone

This stage is more like a bridge from the old to the new. Students are still attached to the old college environment while trying to adapt to the new college environment. An example of this phase might be a student taking final exams and getting ready for graduation at their community college while registering for the right courses to take during their first semester or finding a place to live on or off campus at the new university.

Managing the change is imperative at this stage as you are getting the new polices and processes at the new university. While you should expect some uncertainty and confusion, you should also remember that there are trained professionals there to answer your questions.

During the Neutral Zone stage you may experience:

- low morale and low productivity.

- anxiety about your role, status or identity at the new school.

- skepticism about how you will fit in and be successful in your new environment.

To help ease this transition, you can:

- meet with your new advisors to confirm that you are on track.

- establish your personal and academic goals for the upcoming semester.

- start building relationships with fellow students and peer advisors.

- attend campus programs/events and begin carving out your place on the campus.

- attend a "time management" workshop to help find balance.

Stage 3: New Beginnings

In this last stage you will experience acceptance and a newly found energy. You will begin to feel a sense of accomplishment and the rewards for your hard work. This is where you will begin to embrace the change. As you begin to experience the energy and motivation related to the adoption of the change, you must also find ways to sustain it.

During the New Beginnings stage you may experience:

- high energy.

- openness to learning.

- renewed commitment to your goals.

To sustain your momentum you can:

- keep your personal and academic goals visible.
- stay organized.
- continue cultivating the new relationships that you have formed.
- celebrate your small wins and reward yourself for your hard work.
- attend student success programs/workshops.
- join a new club or organization—get involved on campus.

Remember that everyone goes through the phases at their own pace. You may move quickly or sometimes feel stuck. This road may be bumpy at times and you may even make some mistakes along the way. Change can be difficult. It requires self-motivation and a strong commitment to your success.

Creating an Action Plan

You have now made your final decision on where you will finish your education. Do you have an action plan for the next few critical steps you need to take? Here is a list of items that you should be sure to complete once you have decided which transfer college/university you will attend.

- Use the formal process of accepting admission to notify the four-year college/university in writing that you have decided to attend.
- Have an official copy of your final grades sent to your transfer college/university.
- Contact campus housing to reserve your space.
- Contact your new faculty advisor for your major to schedule your first official advising session.
- Contact the admissions and the college business office to find out when tuition, fees, and housing deposits are due and how they must be paid.
- Sign up for New and Transfer Student Orientation.

Take a minute to work through the table below of the next 3-5 tasks you need to complete as you begin your transfer process. There are some ideas listed below to get you started. Also, try to incorporate applicable tasks from the college road map. You can complete your own transition plan on Exercise 7.2 at the end of this chapter.

Table 1: Transfer Task List

Action Item	Dates	Notes	Complete/ Incomplete
Attend community college and receive a _____ degree.	August 2013 – May 2015		
I will transfer to _____ where I will major in _____.	August 2015 – May 2017		
Attend transfer student orientation.			

What If It Doesn't Work Out?

It is possible that you may get to your senior university and things may not work out as planned. Maybe you have issues with your finances, family obligations or other life events that prevent you from completing your education at that school. Make sure that before you choose to leave, you exhaust every effort to make it work. Try using some of the student support services available to you at the university. For academic issues, meet with your professor and look into tutoring. For financial issues you may want to look into part-time work or unclaimed scholarships. If you have trouble with your roommate or living in the residence halls, the Housing Office can help you resolve roommate conflicts or secure other housing arrangements.

If none of these resolve your issue and you find that it is best to leave, don't feel like a failure. Take whatever steps you need to take to exit that institution with dignity and go to your Plan B scenario. Take care to ensure you have withdrawn from your courses if necessary and spoken to your advisors and counselors. You will want to make sure you leave in good standing and that such good standing is reflected on your academic record. You can then take your experiences, learn from those and move to your Plan B as soon as you are able. Also, find out if you are eligible for a refund of your tuition and fees. The money can help you get started on Plan B.

Final Thoughts

Our journey to transferring successfully has come to an end. But in reality this is just the beginning: the beginning of a new chapter in your life, your mission and your educational journey. We hope that the information and techniques learned in this course will provide you with the knowledge and confidence to successfully transition into a four-year college/university environment.

Additionally, we hope that this transition will help bring to fruition your goals of graduating with a bachelor's degree and your successful entry into the career of your choice and living your best life. While you will have many people you can go to for advice such as advisors, counselors, friends and family, we hope you will realize you have the power to create the kind of future you want.

"Your time is limited, so don't waste it living someone else's life. Don't let the noise of others' opinions drown out your own inner voice. And most important, have the courage to follow your heart and intuition." – Steve Jobs.

Quick Tips for Academic Success

With some help from the authors of "College Student Success," Bazan, J., Bazan, L., Dunham and Johnson, we have outlined the following "Academic Success Strategies" to help you flourish in college:

1. **Go to class:** Set the tone of academic success from day one of classes. Be there. Pay no attention to the falsehood that it's okay to miss the first day of class because no important work will be covered. On the first day you meet your professor and classmates, find out the course objectives, discover what the expectations are, and have an opportunity ask the professor any questions you have. Attendance is also an important part of your overall grade in your classes. Missing classes can result in a point deduction from your final grade. If you have to miss a class due to illness or an emergency, always contact your professor in advance to arrange submitting homework due on the day you miss and how you can make up work covered in class.

2. **Manage your time wisely:** The skill of managing your time effectively while in college is a must. It is important to your success as a student. Effective time management is a conscious decision in which you decide what is important and then plan your time and your life around these things. It increases your productivity and helps decrease your stress level while promoting student success. Play a proactive role by knowing what your goals are, getting organized and planning in advance.

   - Use a calendar/planner and write everything down in one place. Be flexible and learn to expect the unexpected. Make a daily "To Do" list and prioritize it.

   - Prioritize what needs to be done, organize, and write down assignment due dates as well as your exam schedule. Schedule time to work on major projects throughout the semester and create realistic deadlines.

   - Find balance. Know your limits and be not afraid to say "NO".

   - Don't forget to make room for entertainment, friends and relaxation. Remember, you are not meant to concentrate on one thing to the exclusion of all else.

3. **Be prepared:** Be prepared to commit your full, uninterrupted attention to the dynamics of the class so that you can extract the important information you need for discussions and future exams. Make sure that you have your textbook on the first day of class. You should have a notebook dedicated to each of your individual classes, extra pens, pencils and highlighters. Make sure that you have pre-read your chapter before class. Write down questions you have about the reading. Underline key concepts, important dates or numbers. Circle or highlight specific examples and significant details that you need to remember. Take summarizing notes in the margins. Pre-reading will also make for great class discussion.

4. **Get to know your professor/instructor:** One of the best ways to become successful in any course is to get to know your instructor. On the first day of class introduce yourself to your professor. Use this opportunity to ask how you can be successful in the class, share your learning style and inquire about the professor's teaching style. Also take the initiative to meet with your professor half way through the class for a progress report.

5. **Identify your learning style:** It is important to your academic success that you identify the best way for you to receive and learn new information. There are three main learning styles. Visual learners are people who tend to learn better by observing and seeing information. They remember information most effectively by vividly seeing information, pictures and takings notes while the professor is lecturing. Kinesthetic Learners are the hands-on learners. They need to be active while learning information rather than listening to a lecture or watching demonstrations.

   Auditory learners learn best by hearing information aloud. To find out what your learning style is, contact your academic advisor or take the VARK questionnaire free online at: www.vark-learn.com/english/page.asp?p=questionnaire

   Once you know what your learning style is, use it. Find instructors who teach to your learning style. You should also learn to embrace other learning styles that might align better with the content of a course. For example, an auditory learner could benefit from using a hands-on (Kinesthetic) approach to practice math problems.

6. **Become engaged in your learning:** Be an active participant in classroom learning. Volunteer for discussion. Students who sit in the front of the class are more likely to be involved in lecture, classroom discussions and activities. This is a great way to show your professors you understand what you are learning in the class and are able to apply it to real-life situations. Don't be afraid to ask questions during class and seek opportunities to confirm you are understanding the material.

7. **Take notes:** Even if you are an auditory learner, you can benefit from the kinesthetic and visual experience of taking notes in class. To most effectively take notes you must be properly rested, alert and engaging your best listening skills. Develop a note taking style that is conducive to your learning style. Explore the different note taking methods and decide which will work best for you and each of your classes. Also, compare your notes to other students in the class. Note the topic areas that are unclear to you and document your questions. You can meet with your professor after class or during their office hours to gain clarification. Always read up on the topic your professor will be lecturing on before your class. This will help make your note taking easier. Prepare for exams from the first day of class.

8. **Study smart:** Identify the time of day when you are most alert. This will be the best time for you to study. Choose a location that is relaxing and quiet. This will minimize distractions and maximize your concentration and ability to focus. Study your difficult subjects and material first. Take a few minutes to outline a study plan to help you stay organized during your study session. This will help you organize topics, study notes and the levels of difficulty for the content to be covered. Use your learning style and take breaks when needed. Here are a few more helpful tips:

   - Prepare for exams from the first day of class.
   - Clean up your notes or re-write notes after each lecture. Review them every other day.
   - Review old tests/quizzes and self-test your knowledge.
   - Use the instructor's clues to the information likely to appear on exams.
   - Form a study group.

- Use different types of studying methods.
- Don't procrastinate and never cram for exams.

9. **Start building your network today:** When you are ready to apply for admission to a four-year university or for future employment, you may be asked for a recommendation. Start building your network of people who are able to attest to your quality of work, dedication and dependability. Building relationships is where you begin.

10. **Be able to identify essential college resources:** This means finding out the locations of all student support services. You need to know where to go if you begin to experience challenges learning information in class. Find out where tutoring services are. If you need help paying for supplies and textbooks, a job might be in order. Career Services is a great place to get help finding employment. You should also know where the Financial Aid and Student Life offices are located. There are many offices that exist on college campuses to help you be successful. Make it a practice to know where these offices are.

11. **Always have access to your student handbook/code of conduct:** You should always know where to find the college policies that apply to your status as a student on whatever college campus you decide to attend. You need to be familiar with the academic integrity policy, the code of conduct and honor codes that may be a part of your campus culture.

12. **Evaluate:** Take the time at the end of every semester to evaluate your progress. This is an opportunity to learn from your successes and from your mistakes. Determine what worked and what didn't work. Revisit your goals to make sure that you stay on target. Document the areas that need improving.

Exercise 7.1: Academic Success Checklist

I. College Services and Important Contacts

Do you know how to access college services at your community college? Document in the chart below where these services are located and any staff members you have worked with.

Resource	Location/Staff Member Contact
Financial Aid	
Advising/Faculty advisor	
Registration	
Tutoring	
Library Services	
Computer labs	
Counseling Services	
Student Life	
Career Services	

List your professors/instructors, their contact information and office hours.

Name and Office Location	Phone	Email	Office hours

Name two fellow classmates you can use for support and list their contact information.

Name	Phone	Email

II. Academic Success Readiness

Below is a list of tasks that successful students do. Read through each one and mark "Yes" or "No." Ask yourself, "Do I....?"

Task	Yes	No
Attend class regularly?		
Come prepared to class?		
Take effective notes?		
Plan my time effectively?		
Have a positive attitude?		
Get involved on campus?		
Know a faculty or staff member who can write a letter of recommendation for me?		
Check in with instructors and classmates when I miss class?		
Prepare effectively for tests and exams?		
Know my learning style?		
Know how to calculate my GPA?		
Know the Code of Conduct Policy at my college?		
Know the Standards of Academic Progress at my college?		

Based on the checklist above, write down three areas that you would like to improve on to become a more successful student and how you plan to improve those skills.

III. Additional Resources

Here are some additional resources to help you with further assessing your learning strategies and study skills. Choose one to two options below to explore.

Resources:

1. Any other Academic related (ACA) classes at your college
2. Resources at your college's Academic Learning Center
3. www.academictips.org/acad/index.html
4. www.dus.psu.edu/academicsuccess/studyskills.html
5. www.dartmouth.edu/~acskills/success/learninglinks.html
6. www.collegesuccess1.com

Exercise 7.2: Create Your Own Personal Mission Statement

Now that you have an idea of what a personal mission statement is and how it is designed, you will create your own. Refer back to your responses to the "Asking Yourself the Right Questions" worksheet for inspiration and create a four to five sentence personal mission statement.

Your Personal Mission Statement:

Next you will establish one long-term goal, two mid-term and two short-term goals that support and are directly related to your personal mission statement. Remember, a long-term goal is a goal to be accomplished in five or more years. A mid-term goal can be accomplished in one to five years, and a short-term goal can be accomplished in one year or less. Think of this task in terms of your long-term goal being related to your career and your mid-term goals being related to the education that will help prepare you for this career. Your short-term goals should be related to your semester here at the community college or your next semester. Focus on using the S.M.A.R.T. process when establishing your goals. This means goals must be specific, measurable, attainable, realistic and timely.

Long-term Goals:

1.

2.

Mid-term Goals:

1.

2.

Short-term Goals:

1.

2.

As you look back on your personal mission statement and goals, what are some tasks that you can commit to doing this week in order to be successful in accomplishing your goals?

How is the selection of your #1 college going to help you achieve your mission?

Exercise 7.3: Transfer Task List

You have now made your final decision on where you will finish your education. Do you have an action plan for the next few critical steps you need to take? Take a minute to work through the table below of the next three to five tasks you need to complete as you begin your transfer process.

Action Item	Dates	Notes	Complete/ Incomplete

Chapter 7 Reflection: Making the Transition

As you complete this chapter, take a moment to reflect on what you discovered and how you can apply it to your goals.

1. What is the benefit of establishing your mission and goals? How can this apply to your educational endeavors and to your life after college?

2. After taking this class, do you feel better prepared to successfully transition to a four-year college/university? Why?

3. What are the three most beneficial things that you learned in this class?

4. What are three things you can do once you are at a four-year college to ensure your successful degree completion?